T0194109

111 Ways to Let Go
of Painful Relationships

111 Ways to Let Go of Painful Relationships

Gay Fry

iUniverse, Inc.
Bloomington

111 WAYS TO LET GO OF PAINFUL RELATIONSHIPS

iUniverse books may be ordered through booksellers or by contacting:
iUniverse
1663 Liberty Drive
Bloomington, IN 47403
www.iuniverse.com
1-800-Authors (1-800-288-4677)

Because of the dynamic nature of the Internet, any web addresses or
links contained in this book may have changed since publication and
may no longer be valid. The views expressed in this work are solely those
of the author and do not necessarily reflect the views of the publisher,
and the publisher hereby disclaims any responsibility for them.

Any people depicted in stock imagery provided by Thinkstock are
models, and such images are being used for illustrative purposes only.

Certain stock imagery © Thinkstock.

ISBN: 978-1-4759-7874-2 (sc)
ISBN: 978-1-4759-7876-6 (hc)
ISBN: 978-1-4759-7875-9 (e)

Printed in the United States of America

iUniverse rev. date: 3/19/2013

I dedicate this book to my mother, aunts, cousins, and awesome women I have known. This book is for anyone who already has or still needs the strength to dig deeply to find his or her spirit. May we all support each other and stand strong as individuals and as a group. May the talents and power of each person help create a more beautiful, peaceful, and loving world. Together we can make a difference. We can take charge and make change. Let us teach the children of tomorrow about peace, calm, loyalty, and respect as we feel these qualities grow within us and shine from our being. Let your light shine.

Acknowledgments

I am very grateful that I have a family (mom, dad, brother, sister, nieces, cousins, aunts and uncles) who has always believed in me. Special thanks go to my sister-in-law, Cheri Irwin, for her artistic talent and for painting my cover. I sincerely appreciate all my good friends and clients who bought copies of my first printing and Alexandra who promoted me and my book. I would like to thank Shifra Miller, David and the James family, Annie Benefield-Lawrence, Jan Miller, Mary Lynch, Kathi Greenaway, Marla Brucker, Beverly Banks Kannowski, Blanca Champa, Donna Shott, Andrea Ania (friend and editor), Duduzile Phindile Mashinini, Mary Linton, as well as my students, clients, and everyone at Vitality—Better Massage Inc. and Vitality College of Healing Arts for their positive reinforcement. A special thanks to my old friends from Braniff, Piedmont, US Airways, New York University, Johns Hopkins University, University of California-San Diego, Oregon State University, Tarrant County College, Alpena Community College, and my wonderful hometown support in Alpena, Michigan. I cannot thank enough my best friend, Julie dog, who kept my feet on the ground until her passing. Big hugs to Tara dog who is a great companion and always makes me smile. Last but not least, I would like to thank the men who were my teachers. I would like to thank my ex-husband and ex-boyfriends. I would never have found the woman I am or learned to appreciate her without the pain that took me to the innermost depth of my being. Suffering gave me my lessons and gave me this book to share with others. God gave me the strength to see it all through and come out smiling on the other side.

111 Ways to Let Go of Painful Relationships

I have paid the price for speaking out.
I have paid the price for keeping silent.
My heart yearns to sing.
My soul yearns to write.
I want to share the way of my journey:
111 ways to let go of painful relationships
And come out whole.

I originally used the techniques I am sharing to help myself let go of a painful marriage and divorce. However, I learned that all of life is about relationships. It is about our relationships with family, friends, work, community, nature, country, animals, pets, the opposite sex, the whole world, and, most importantly, ourselves. Within our heart and soul we carry hopes, dreams, ideals, and emotions for all of these relationships. As you have probably noticed, these relationships come not only with love and joy but also with pain and heartache. We are not usually taught how to deal with the pain and heartache parts of life's relationships.

A company for which I had worked for over fourteen

years went bankrupt. I loved my job and was emotionally invested. I had expected to be there until I was too old to show up. Instead, the company filed for bankruptcy, and I received a telegram that my job had been eliminated. I heard most of the information on the afternoon news. Losing my job after fourteen years made me feel lost as a person. I could not use my company ID which left me confused as to who I was and where to go next.

I was afraid of divorce, so I waited until I was forty-two to get married, thinking I would be much smarter then and would do it right. Waiting and fear did not make me wiser, and I had a horrible marriage. Thank God it ended without ruining my health. With the loss of my marriage, I lost hopes and dreams I had held since childhood. I also lost friends, family, and things that I thought were important.

In the past few years I have lost my mother, father, and some close relatives. Losing parents leaves a deep void and starts an emotional roller coaster that is a book in itself. I lost my dear dog Julie who was with me for sixteen years. I have had to move many times and lose friends and all that was comfortable and familiar. I have learned a lot from these losses. I learned that life is full of change. I learned that fear was my only enemy and that my thirst for knowledge and adventure was my best friend. I also learned that I am a survivor; I know I will do what it takes to survive. I developed a friendship with the deepest part of myself. I trust myself—I will always have me. I also have faith that whatever happens is always going to turn out to be for my good.

Whenever I heard about women so trapped in their fear, anger, and sense of betrayal that they would kill someone or seek revenge in some horrendous way, I knew I had to share my journey. I drove into a strip mall one day and my soon-to-be ex was right there in front of me. I was tempted to step on the gas, but I had set in my mind how to pull out of anger and think immediately of God and nature. I realized that my husband would have ended up with God and I would have ended up in jail. I let go of that anger immediately. I was learning how to put my happiness and well-being first. My relationship to God, nature, and primarily myself, gave me an inner strength that took me through a four and a half year divorce and helped me find a new career and a new life. The skills I used have taken me through many painful losses, the most recent of which was my mother.

I accept the fact that life changes and these changes can be painful, but I cry, I use my techniques, and I am ready for what comes next. I have learned that I am blessed, so I just let the blessings flow. If you accept that you are blessed, then you are.

I also had to accept that my way of thinking and my coping skills needed an overhaul. I had issues. I made up my mind that I would not worry about my ex and what he was doing, that I would instead concentrate on healing myself. My heart, soul, and whole being were all in pain. I now work on myself and do what makes me happy, and I love my life. I felt a need for classes and therapies, which would ultimately give me the tools to heal myself.

Core beliefs, logic, reality, and spirituality have done battle. The following 111 ways to let go of painful relationships helped me not only to survive but also to emerge with a whole new life and a whole new me. It was my private investigator, Oscar, who suggested I share my techniques for survival with other women. He told me he was impressed by my strength and that I did not waste my energy on useless anger. I worked at staying centered and growing both spiritually and as a woman.

I used to believe it was a woman's duty to keep the marriage together, and I was willing to die to make my marriage last. When I could not save the marriage, I had to interview lawyers. Many of them questioned me about the care of my husband, intimating that if the marriage had failed it was because I did not take care of my husband's sexual needs. Not once did anyone ask if I had been happy in the marriage. No one asked if *my* sexual needs or any other needs had been met. I believe society convinced me that my needs did not matter. Only now, after a lot of work on myself, do I see that I have a right to expect my needs to be met. Not only did my needs take last place, but so did my feelings. I really thought everyone's feelings were more important than mine. I would say to myself, *you're strong, what does it matter.* The big realization is that it *did* matter. Every time I put myself last, not only did I teach others to put me last, but also a little bit of me was wounded; the pain added up over time.

As I look back, I realize there never really was a marriage. We had a beautiful wedding. It was my dream wedding. However, immediately after the wedding, my husband changed. When we entered our hotel room, he started yelling at me about what I should do with my wedding dress. He did not make sense, and I knew I had made a mistake. Since this was my first marriage and I was forty-two, I was afraid everyone would think I had the wedding jitters. I decided to go on the honeymoon and deal with it when I returned. I had no idea how to communicate my feelings about his behavior. We went to New York and then to Egypt. On our honeymoon, I could do nothing right. I did not know how to hold hands or even walk. He found fault with everything I did. It seems marriage made me stupid and, in a way, I guess it did.

I see that I had stayed single, in spite of countless marriage proposals, because of a fear of divorce. I had attracted what I feared.

What amazes me more than how my husband treated

me and lied to me is how I lied to myself. I convinced myself I could make it work. I believed in my Christmas card with the picture of us looking like the perfect couple. In order to keep up this façade, I wore rose-colored glasses. I wore these glasses for seven and a half years as I dedicated myself to our business and buried myself in work and classes. I was told and believed that if I worked hard we would retire together in comfort. The rose-colored glasses prevented me from seeing who my husband really was and what a sham my life was. I convinced myself that I was deeply in love with this man who clearly did not have my well-being anywhere on his list of cares and concerns, let alone his priority list. I felt trapped and was experiencing the Stockholm syndrome, identifying with and protecting my captor. Feeling trapped caused me to love this man who felt like my evil captor. I believed my survival depended on going along with and protecting him. I never let anyone know how he treated me. Little did I know that almost everyone saw who he was except me.

I have worked with many men and women who have died of cancer or other degenerative diseases to escape their marriages. I believe that deep down they felt as I did, that death was the only way out. It is true that an unhappy marriage can lead to serious health issues.

When I realized there was no way to save the marriage and divorce was imminent, the rose-colored glasses melted away like magic. I began to see everything as if someone had been taking notes for seven and a half years and handed them to me. I knew then I had to let go and move on. I had to let go of the life I thought I was living and admit I was living a lie. It was time to look deep inside and find the truth. It was time to look at how I got here and to start over.

It was a fragile time; however, my support system was God, nature, and my Julie dog. You cannot get much larger than that, but my husband totally underestimated my support system. Mates like mine do what they can to alienate you from other people. They find fault with your family and friends and with any time you spend with them. If you are totally reliant on them, they are in control.

During my four and a half year divorce, many women emailed or telephoned me for advice. How they found out about me and my struggle for equality in the judicial system, I will never know. I hope I helped them, for they helped me see that I am much more powerful than I thought. This power did not help in the courtroom, however. The "good ole boy" system still exists in many courtrooms across the country, and gender bias does not elude even the most progressive states. My inner strength served to help me get past, yet not ignore, the treatment of women and myself in our court system. The indisputable power we give our judges is not only scary but needs reevaluation.

Being a yoga teacher, doula (someone who nurtures women during labor and delivery), hypnotherapist, labyrinth facilitator, massage teacher, hypnosis teacher, international flight attendant, cancer therapist, and just a good listener, I have heard some incredible life stories. I worked with one woman who could not go two minutes without talking about her ex-husband, the divorce, the new wife, or their lifestyle. She was consumed with the activities of her ex because another woman had taken on her role in life and she wanted her part back. She had played her part well and expected reward. Instead, she was replaced. She felt like this man had just replaced her with an ingénue, a new and younger woman, and she did not understand how it all happened. She felt out of control and could not put herself back in her life role. With no awareness of her true beauty and talent, she developed cancer immediately and died at a very young age. She had lost herself as a person when she took on the role of the perfect wife. She did not have her real self to fall back on after she lost the role upon which she worked so hard for so long.

I have worked with young men and women who were not married, yet could not recover from a break up. They did not feel lovable; therefore, they beat themselves up for their failed relationships. Some of them actually became unable to function in life. Some lost or quit their jobs, feeling like social outcasts. I know how they feel, and I know what it takes to get over it. The empty, useless, lost, ugly, and discarded feeling that unhealthy relationships leave you with drowns you in a well of deep abandonment. Feeling abandoned by others and full of self-loathing, we abandon ourselves. I have been there with friends, family, clients, and myself. It is difficult to see clearly when you are in the thick of it, and I hope this book helps you find your way out. It is important to learn respect for yourself and your life's journey. Get out of the relationship the best way you can and take time to find out who you are. Spend time learning to like and protect yourself. Reestablish trust in yourself and your choices. Then you will not *need* anyone. This can lead to a healthy relationship with yourself and others. First, let us become free! Freedom is your birthright.

If these steps sound like they are written for women, it is because I am a woman and I have had my experience from a woman's standpoint. I have also worked with men and been assured that there are women like my husband and men like me. There are men who have experienced marriage the way I did. In these cases, please substitute the word *woman* or *mate* where it is applicable. I hope we can teach young men and women to have quality relationships and live with a great quality of life. I wish only happiness, love, peace, and good health for everyone.

> "The greatest discovery of all time is that a person can change his future by merely changing his attitude." –*Oprah Winfrey*

Safe Place—Create a safe place. If you were in a painful relationship, you most likely did not feel safe. It has been my experience that most people do not feel safe in the world; hence, the inner tension is often heightened by the outer tension. If you were involved with a "crazy maker," you may have lived the tension of walking on eggshells. Be aware of creating a safe place for yourself. A safe place can be one room, a closet, garage, bathroom, whole house, or a place you go in your imagination. Where the mind goes, the energy flows. Do not underestimate what you can do with your imagination.

Some people have never felt safe in their lives with anyone anywhere. Spend time connecting with your soul and your body. This time with yourself can be the greatest gift you give yourself. I was fortunate enough to have a whole house for my dog and me. I had worked hard all my life including during my marriage. Working morning, noon, and night enabled me to keep blinders on and not have time to see how unhealthy my situation was. When everything started to come out into the open, my Julie dog and I started feeling safer immediately. I could feel myself unfold as if I were coming out of a cocoon.

Once you get the feeling of being safe inside yourself, you are ready to learn how to feel safe in the outside world. That can be a little harder and take a little longer. Remember you have a lifetime, so just go one day at a time. Be gentle and patient with yourself. Keep yourself safe until you have your wings and all your healthy color. You will then fly away free! You can train yourself to realize that peace and calm are safe. Chaos and tension are neither safe nor healthy.

If you are or were living with an abusive person, maybe you need to relocate. Your physical safety is most important. When you are physically safe you can then begin to work on your mental and emotional safety.

Below is a safe place meditation. You can use it almost anywhere, including the dentist's office, doctor's office, or while you're waiting to have your tires rotated. I teach this technique to expectant moms to use during childbirth. It also works for children. Feel free to share it. Please do not use it while driving, tending small children or operating machinery.

Safe Place Meditation

Make yourself comfortable in a quiet place where you will not be disturbed. You can be in silence or use peaceful, relaxing New Age music. Close your eyes and beneath your lids look up as far as you can. Then just let your eyes relax as you take three long, slow, deep breaths, breathing all the way down to your navel. Allow yourself to feel light and free. Use your imagination to picture yourself on a large bluff overlooking the ocean. Let all of your senses be there. Smell and taste the salty air as you feel the ocean breeze on your face. Then take the nice, gentle path off to the side that leads down to the beach. You can create a beautiful safe place here on the beach, or you can take a path inland where you can create your own beautiful garden. Let your imagination go as you choose flowers, trees, ponds, fish, and other garden decorations. A hammock or chaise lounge is nice. Build a dwelling of any size and have boats of any size. The more details the better.

I had a client who built a sweet, small house in her imagination, and each time she visited, she took time to water her flowers. She had many flowers in her safe place. One lady liked to get a massage on the beach; one had a yacht where she sat in the hot tub drinking champagne. Some like to swim with the dolphins, while others go inland where there are mountains and animals near a charming cabin. With practice, you can allow yourself to go there for ten, fifteen, or thirty minutes and come back. This technique will alleviate stress, which will help you reach peace, calm, good decision-making, and good health. When you relax and go into your imagination, your body's own intelligence can help heal itself. This is just one of many ways you can teach yourself to relax and let go of fears and anxiety.

2

Garage Sale or Charity—A garage sale is a fun way to let go. The old stuff has connections to the old life. Let it go. You can chat with neighbors and make a little fun money. Since it always feels good to give, you can then take the rest to charity, or give it all to charity. Whatever you do, the act of getting rid of things and rearranging your living space will help reaffirm your freedom. Let go of the stuff and let go of the person connected to the stuff. Everything is replaceable except you, your health and well-being. Letting go of stuff is an important part of freeing yourself up to move on.

"Some of us think holding on makes us strong; but sometimes it is letting go."—Hermann Hesse

3

De-clutter—Getting rid of clutter and simplifying your life can take a lot of weight off your shoulders. Having lots of stuff requires lots of work and lots of space. Free yourself and have more space to breathe and create your new life. I had a huge garage sale and put tons of stuff out for the trash, which was mostly taken away by neighbors or passersby. I have given so much away that I am more conscientious of what I purchase, knowing someday I will have to deal with it or give it away. I sent truckloads to my favorite charities. I know a lady who impresses me with her ability to live clutter free. She has no qualms about giving away anything she does not use often. I am still working on this one but getting better every day. De-cluttering also means getting organized. I continue to work on this one, too. If you need help Andrew J. Mellen's Book *Unstuff Your Life!: Kick the Clutter Habit and Completely Organize Your Life for Good*, could help get you on your way. Sometimes we need the extra guidance we can get from a book or professional living in your area.

4

Simplify—simplify, simplify, simplify. I cannot stress enough the importance of simplifying your life and making it livable. I remember seeing a movie in which a woman got a divorce and moved to a small house. The inside was sparse and clutter-free with a few nice pieces. As I watched, I felt the peace it must have given her, and I longed for an equally simple life. Simplicity is always my goal. I also examine why I feel the need to do so much in life. I am still a work in progress. Simplifying your life can give you room to explore yourself and develop the inner you. Technique numbers 2, 3 and 4 seem alike but trust me when I say they are different. They need serious, positive attention and need to be revisited every couple of years. The reward is that afterward you will feel light and free. Francine Jay has written some help for you with the book, *The Joy of Less, A Minimalist Living Guide: How to Declutter, Organize, and Simplify Your Life.*

5

Redecorate the bedroom—Redecorate the house, especially the bedroom. Paint the walls. Get new sheets. Make your living space and your bedroom reflect *you*, as a woman in charge of her life. Make it comfortable for you to snuggle up, read, lie in bed on Saturday mornings, and create dreams for your new life. Remember, if you can dream it, you can make it come true.

Visions are a function of the right side of the brain, which is more powerful than the left side. Left brain functions include speech, which is why you can talk about something, but it won't happen unless you can visualize it. For example, if you say, "I will never eat chocolate cake again," but in your mind you imagine a beautiful chocolate cake, chances are you will be eating chocolate cake. Therefore, imagine yourself feeling happy and fulfilled. See yourself happy. Relax in the happy feeling.

If money is tight, shuffle your furniture around, trade with friends, or hit flea markets. I have had awesome luck with flea markets and garage sales.

6

Children—If children are involved, get counseling. Change is hard on adults but even harder on children. They thrive on routine. They will need more attention than usual and want reassurance that they are loved. Books and movies about divorces that work out are very good. Do not ask them to choose sides. They love you both and are a part of each of you. If you slander your partner, children will take it personally and also feel slandered. If your ex plays games, says awful things about you, or uses the children, do not join in. Remember, you are setting an example of how to live. Your strength and dignity will serve both you and your children well. It is important to spend time with your children. Go to the zoo, have a picnic, go to the library, and read books together. Be the source of peace, safety, healing, and joy for your children, not the source of pain. The most valuable thing you can give a child is your time.

My ex was playing awful mind games with our godchildren; therefore, I had to stop seeing them. I could not bear to watch them parrot what they were told. To me, it was better if they thought I abandoned them instead of believing the horrible things they were fed. I knew they would have been fed nothing if I hadn't been in the picture. My ex wanted to hurt me, but I felt it hurt the children more.

I realize you do not want to walk away from your children. Just be aware of the games and vow not to play.

There are some wonderful books on divorce for children as well as support groups for single parents. There is nothing like information to give you confidence and peace of mind. Many helpful books exist such as: *Putting Children First: Proven Parenting Strategies for Helping Children Thrive Through Divorce* by JoAnne Pedro-Carroll, *The Truth about Children and Divorce: Dealing With Emotions So You and Your Children Can Thrive* by Robert Emery, *Two Homes* by Clair Masurel and Kady MacDonald Denton, *Divorce Poison New and Updated Edition: How to Protect Your Family from Bad-mouthing and Brainwashing* by Dr. Richard A. Warshak. These are just a few from which you can find what will work best for you and your situation.

7

Old Friends—If there is big money involved in a divorce, it has been my experience that most people will follow the money. Money is power, and they both rule. Many male judges do not think business and women go together. You may have been the brains and earned the money. You may have worked very hard, but do not expect that to be acknowledged. You may have worked hard at the business while your spouse was having affairs, but do not expect anyone to care. Be prepared to start over in all areas of your life.

There is a very strong possibility you will be all alone during your breakup and divorce. This can be a good thing. It is time to learn to be your own best friend and spend quality time with yourself. You will also learn who your true friends are. In many divorces, one person lies. They know this throws the partner off and can cause them to do crazy things. Then they sit with innocent looks on their faces. Only those who have dealt with this kind of "crazy maker" realize who is telling the truth. You have to know who you are by sitting in your truth and not reacting. Those who believe the "crazy maker" are not enlightened enough to be in your new world, so breathe and let them go. I know it is not as easy as it sounds.

It can be especially painful if you worked hard, thinking you were doing it for your family and marriage, just to find out your spouse did not have the same fidelity or loyalty. You may feel emotionally and physically invested because of your labor, but it may be time to let it go. Nothing is worth the sacrifice of your health and happiness.

Happiness is a choice, and good health comes with happiness. My spirituality and these 111 steps kept me sane. I was single for forty-two years and even though I lost myself in my marriage, deep down I knew who I was. I had been with just myself and survived a long time. I knew this was just a test. I am a survivor and have strong faith. I have no doubt that I am guided and blessed. I not only know it but I feel it in every cell of my being. I know I will be fine and end up where I need to be. I have friends in high places.

"It is not the strongest of the species that survives, nor the most intelligent but the one most responsive to change."—Attributed to Charles Darwin

8

New Friends—It is important to get out and join new groups and establish new friendships. You can start a group if you cannot find one. I have created groups of women who just like to get together and share their thoughts and ideas. This evolved into a group of women who share their dreams. We take turns stating our hearts' desires, and then we all visualize our dreams and create space for them. It is empowering. You can have a group of women who like tea, like to knit, or are looking for new careers. Any common or uncommon goal will work because most women need someone to listen. It's all about having a voice and being heard.

Research has shown that men fare better in a marriage and women fare better being single. A Time Magazine article by Ayanna Buyhto was titled, "Is Marriage Better for Men Than Women? News Reports Say, Yes" and printed in January 21, 2010. Many women keep in their thoughts and feelings. As Archie Bunker said in *All in the Family*, "stifle Edith!" As a massage therapist I can feel all the held in words and feelings. I share techniques with my clients on how to let go, breathe and feel lighter and happier.

9

Cover Your Assets—It is important to know where the money is. Make sure everything is in your name as well as your spouse's. Make copies of important paperwork. Many times a spouse will hide assets. You will need proof in the courtroom. To start over you will need a bank account, credit union, and assets in your name. It is always good to keep accounts in your name no matter how long you have been together or how great the relationship. Many of us step back, content to be the woman behind the man. We get so far behind that our vision is blocked and we cannot see where we are going. It is best to keep things in your name when you get married. I have heard of men never putting their wife's name on deeds to property and during divorce, pretending that it does not exist. Suze Orman has many books to help give you the information you will need. *Women & Money: Owning the Power to Control Your Destiny* and *The Money Class: How to Stand in Your Truth and Create the Future You Deserve* are just two to consider.

10

Financial Planning—Make a plan. Do not rely on credit cards. The credit card industry is about profit and not about you. They will stop your credit but continue to charge you huge fees. Treating a credit card like "money in the bank" can wreak havoc on your credit and peace of mind for a long time. Your lifestyle may change drastically but do not get caught in a trap of deep debt.

Many women fall to poverty level after divorces because some men and women want to punish their ex-spouses more than they want to protect their children. I am appalled at how many men leave their families with nothing, only to go out and start another family. I remember a man who was very angry because he wanted his wife to go out and sell makeup and she wanted to stay home to take care of their baby boy. When I questioned him, he told me of his promise to take care of her so she could be a stay-at-home mom. He had wanted his son to have the benefit of a mom being there for him at all times. However, his anger at his wife became more important than his son's well-being. I am amazed at how anger at another person can cause people to sacrifice their children.

I recommend keeping a bank account in a different

bank or credit union. When my husband and I got married we went to the bank and opened an account together. After we were married awhile, he got a secret password for the account, and I could not touch it. It took a court order to access an account I had opened in person. How does someone get total control of your life? It's very easy to do when you refuse to look at what is happening because you cannot take the truth.

Frontline presented a story on the Public Broadcasting Station titled, "By the Number: Childhood Poverty in the US" and used this information from the United States Census Bureau: "The nation's poorest kids primarily live in households headed by a single female. Nearly half of all children with a single mother—47.6 percent—live in poverty. Indeed, the children of single mothers experience poverty at a rate that is more than four times higher than kids in married-couple families."

This was an awakening view of the plight of single mothers trying to work, feed, provide a roof for and tend to the basic needs of their children. It is also great insight into the effect this plight has on the children. This is a powerful piece and needs to be viewed by everyone in the United States.

Spending—I have observed that people spend their money like they spend their energy. Some waste money and they waste their time. How you spend your money speaks volumes about what kind of person you are. Those too thrifty are often too thrifty with their love, emotions, and all forms of giving. Seek balance. I know people who only feel good about themselves and their lives if they can go out and spend money. This can become an addiction. Like any addiction, spending money can leave you feeling empty at the end of the day. We seek to fill the emptiness inside, and nothing can fill that but self-exploration, which leads to self-love. Feelings of satisfaction and peace are elusive when we substitute emptiness and pain with frivolity instead of working our way through the pain.

Some addictions, such as overworking and the need to please are socially acceptable. An addiction can be destructive, whether it is spending money, overworking, drinking, smoking, having sex, exercising, or eating. Addictions can destroy your health and your relationships. Being unable to establish a relationship with yourself can lead to continued pain and emptiness. Notice what some of your addictions are. I have an addiction to books. I often purchase a book thinking I must have it even though I have not even read my last purchase.

Spending seems to give many people a temporary high and the feeling that they are okay. Many people get caught up in receiving gifts and/or money as a sign that they are loved. Some get caught up in giving. The need to give is another hook that some use to control someone else or to feel bigger than life.

Love and money have nothing to do with each other. Yet, I know some people who think the two are related. I know a woman who panics when there is no man contributing to her expenses. She makes a very healthy salary, yet will not save money. She feels the need to live very large in order to feel like she is somebody.

Love and money are not synonymous. Your self-worth is not to be gauged by your bank account or anyone else's. Marsha Sinetar's book, *Do What You Love, the Money Will Follow: Discovering Your Right Livelihood*. Also, Barbara Sher and Barbara Smith's, *I Could Do anything If I Only Knew What It Was: How to Discover What You Really Want and How to Get It*. You could also try, *The Gifts of Imperfection: Let Go of Who You Think You're Supposed to Be and Embrace Who You Are*, by Brene Brown and *The Courage To Be Yourself: A Woman's Guide to Emotional Strength and Self-Esteem*, by Judith Orloff. I hope we are coming to a time when we value each other by the riches we possess internally rather than externally. True wealth is an internal feeling. When I help a woman birth her baby I feel like the richest woman in the world. I wish I could share that feeling of wealth in this book but it is unexplainable.

> "If a person gets his attitude toward money straight, it will straighten out almost every other area in his life."—Billy Graham

12

Suffering—Suffering and pain can be wonderful gifts. As long as everything is going well, we do not have to dig deep inside ourselves and bring out the real power. I have heard many people say their cancer was a gift. Needless to say, they were cancer survivors.

Some people are only comfortable when they are suffering. Notice if you seem to feel better when your life is in chaos. Are you more comfortable when you complain about your life?

Personally, I work hard to keep my life peaceful and calm. I like to be happy. I have had people mistake my peaceful life for an easy life. It is just as easy to make your life peaceful and calm as it is to make it full of problems and chaos. Choose happiness.

We often make our decisions based on what we think will prevent suffering, only to have them lead to pain and suffering. Our life decisions can be love-based rather than fear-based Oprah has said that most animals run from fear, but we humans seem to keep moving toward fear.

I have been in some countries where I was in unpleasant situations for days on end but I wrote and created beyond my wildest dreams. I found I loved being with myself and I enjoyed exploring the world alone.

Some feel that suffering is the way to God. Suffering has taken me on a pathway closer to God. I have learned that I am never alone.

"Ending suffering requires us to be quiet long enough to see how suffering happens. Quiet is necessary because the clamor of modern life and endless chatter in our heads detracts from our ability to discern the automatic, conditioned, karmic patterns we mistake for who we are. This "mistake," believing ourselves to be less than we are, roars in our ears and captures our vision. As far as I know, silence is the only antidote."–Cheri Huber

Counseling –When going through a divorce or breakup that sends you reeling, seek expert advice whenever and wherever you can. Some cities and colleges provide free classes and clinics. Find out where they are and go. You never know when you may get some helpful advice. Check out local bookstores as well as city, county, and law libraries. It is empowering to go to a law library and understand your rights. Ask for help in finding appropriate resources.

It is important to understand that judges rule and can use the law as they interpret it, so do not always expect fairness or justice. Judges are just people who have marriage problems and get divorced like everyone else. Some are abusers, alcoholics, and have prejudices just like anyone else.

Divorce, letting go, and happiness are all inside jobs. Treat yourself fairly but do not look for fairness elsewhere. Personally, having more information made me feel in charge of my life, and I ended up writing my own trial brief. The judge was able to get rid of my attorney while favoring my husband's two attorneys in an attempt to make me powerless. I heard from a local paralegal that the judge was also in divorce proceedings during my case.

A lot more goes on in judges' chambers than we are privy to. I recommend getting the best lawyer you can if the divorce is not amicable. Ask around to see what names come up; a few names will come up more than once. Stifle your emotions with lawyers and when you're in the courtroom. Give only the facts. Save all emotions for your therapist or journal.

The truth is that no one listens to someone who is overly emotional. People tune you out. Be clear and give only pertinent facts. Unfortunately, liars have a better chance of their voices being heard because there is no emotion with a lie. I have noticed that professionals like Dr. Phil can spot these controlled liars who drive others mad.

14

Set New Goals—It is important to know where you want to go if you expect to get there. The old dreams and old goals are dead. This is an opportunity for positive change. You are now free to downsize and create a nice, simple, fun life for yourself. Get a notebook and get started. Make a list of your dreams and goals to read often. Feel free to make changes as you grow and learn. If you do not know what you want, you cannot attract anything to you. Be clear with yourself about your needs, hopes and desires. This will help you create a reality in which you can thrive. It is important when you wake up each morning to have a purpose and know what that purpose is. A goal can be as simple as noticing when your body is under stress and when it is relaxed. A goal can be as complicated as taking classes for a degree, preparing for the New York marathon, passing the bar exam, writing a book, or owning your own boutique. It can be as dramatic as skydiving or as fun as going for walks to see birds and flowers. Remember, where your mind goes, the energy flows.

"Step by step. I can't think of any other way of accomplishing anything."—Michael Jordan

15

Oprah and Dr. Phil—The Oprah and Dr. Phil shows can give you new tools and ideas by providing free counseling in the privacy of your home where you can cry all you want. It helps to understand you are not alone and to see how others cope. You will also need to regain your self-esteem and see how you got where you are so you can get out and not come back. It is important to honor where you came from and honor all parts of yourself, including the parts you do not like.

Maybe you have habits that you picked up from one of your parents. If you can see where these habits came from, then you can develop compassion for your parents and learn compassion for yourself.

Oprah helped save my life with her life-changing shows, and she continues to enhance my life. Oprah's website often has her workshops, projects, programs, and book recommendations that facilitate emotional and spiritual healing.

Oprah now has her own network called OWN. She is always creating new avenues for those of us with a thirst for growth. I love her Super Soul Sundays. No one can ever replace her, but I do hope others show up to inform, enrich and help transform lives.

16

Get Cyber Smart—Many women are busy with families and have not taken the time to learn how to use a computer. To start your life over, you will need a computer. You may want your own business and website. You can take classes or work from home. You can surf the web for jobs and research just about anything. Cell phones put you in touch with the whole world as well. Everything is getting a little more user-friendly. Some of my precious aunts take adult classes offered by the local community college; they are very good at sending email and skyping.

While searching the internet, I found websites that take judicial complaints. There used to be a committee studying gender bias in the California courts. The committee should be reinstated because there seems to be few checks and balances on the judicial system, something I find quite scary. During the four and a half years of my divorce I felt I was not heard once in the courtroom.

With a computer you can get involved. You can find information on just about any topic. You can find help with investing, moving, selling items, looking for a new job, or locating old friends by just surfing the web. You can make a new friend, plan a trip, and purchase new books and music. You can see what is playing at the local cinema, discover a local restaurant that serves your favorite food or get a new recipe. It is all there at your fingertips.

My favorite thing about the internet is the ability to stay in touch with family and friends no matter where they are in the world. With a webcam you can have coffee with your best friend or relative who resides in another state or country. I love having coffee with my brother in the morning or a beer at the end of the day, and we live at opposite ends of the United States. I can also watch my grandniece color or teach her yoga even though she is over 800 miles away. I love technology. When it works it is amazing.

17

Hold a Wake—When someone dies, we have a ceremony to help survivors move on. Death of a marriage or relationship is the death of hopes, dreams, vows, and deep inner contracts. I recommend putting pictures and mementos into a box and setting it on fire. (Safely, of course) Write and read a eulogy. You might want to read the eulogy many times until you can read it without breaking down. The symbolism involved in watching it all burn to ashes can be very healing. You can do this alone or with a few friends and talk about the good times as well as the bad times, finishing with a toast. Honor the past for the lessons completed and wisdom earned. Honor the future for the new hopes and dreams. I have burned many pictures, smashed a wedding cake topping, tossed objects in the ocean, and to get over it all, I toasted with champagne. It all helped immensely, but grieving still takes time. Be aware of the grieving process and give yourself permission to grieve. I believe the death of a marriage is not given the proper respect. If it were, there would be a lot more emotionally healthy people and maybe fewer divorces. Also, remember this is the death of many hopes and dreams. Mourning is letting go. Grief and loss are high on the stress scale so be sure to get lots of rest and to be gentle with yourself.

> "It's not the load that breaks you down, it's the way you carry it."—Lena Horne

18

Herbs—Check with your doctor first. I have found that the heart really does ache and taking herbs can help. My heart hurt, and I would put my hands over it and talk sweetly to myself to help heal the pain. I bought hawthorn berry herbs and took a capsule a day to help my heart physically and symbolically. I wanted my heart, my soul, and my body to know I understood the pain, and that I wanted to live. I wanted my body to know that I cared about its needs and would support it any way I could.

Heartaches and breakups are very real and take their toll on us physically. It is important to nurture yourself. You will also need extra support for your nervous system and immune system. Many people get cancer or other major illnesses during a breakup or divorce. This is another good reason to make a clean break and move on. Your health cannot afford for you to hang on.

One of my yoga students came to me after class and asked if I could help her. The doctor she had seen for her heart said nothing was wrong but she felt very real pain. I asked what was going on in her life, and she replied that she was getting a divorce and her father was dying. I assured her that this was enough for a heart to be in pain, and I explained how she could nurture and coddle herself a little to help. She informed me later that she felt better not expecting herself to feel so great about all that was going on in her life. She got garlic capsules to help her physically. Her doctor was correct that nothing was physically wrong with her heart, and she just needed some self-nurturing to ease the pain.

While I was married I went to play golf one day with my husband. We were paired with a heart surgeon and his friend. My husband was being his normal self, trying to belittle me and making me feel horrible about myself. The heart surgeon noticed and did everything he could to make me feel special. This put a kink in my husband's nastiness, and he thought the doctor was flirting with me, but I knew exactly what the good doctor was doing. He was reminding me of how I was supposed to be treated. I will never forget it, and I said a prayer of thanks for him when I got home. I have no doubt that this doctor can heal hearts because he understands them on every level. It was also a reminder for me to treasure myself.

Years later I met a young girl of ten who hurt in the area of her heart. The girl said she had felt this pain since she was three years old. Her mother took her to the doctor who assured her there was nothing wrong and that it was probably growing pains. While talking with her I discovered that her parents were divorced when she was three. I explained to her that when she was that young she may not have understood what was happening, but that now, through journaling and help from her mother, she could have a different perspective and possibly heal the pain.

Just yesterday a client told me how she was having heart palpitations and her doctor was giving her all kinds of test. The company she was working for fired her and she was fine. Her job was making her sick because her heart was not in it.

Whenever I have a pain in my body I look to see what my body wants me to know. Pains in our bodies are asking us to stop and take a moment to examine our emotional and spiritual pain as well as physical pain. We are mind, body, and spirit. We must address our whole being for health and well-being.

The answer to happiness, health, and well-being is within. Do not look for love, respect, and approval outside of yourself. The approval, respect, and love must come from within. If you are fortunate enough to meet someone who also shows you approval, respect, and love, it is a wonderful bonus and in no way replaces self-respect, self-approval, and self-love. Be gentle with yourself. I highly recommend reading anything by Dr. Andrew Weil or Dr. Deepak Chopra. I also appreciate Dr. Oz because he is so open-minded and is always searching for ways to teach us how our bodies work and how we can take care of them before seeking professional medical help.

Author of *Molecules of Emotions*, Candace B. Pert Ph.D. says, "A feeling sparked in your mind will translate as a peptide being released somewhere. Peptides regulate every aspect of your body from whether you're going to digest your food properly to whether you're going to destroy a tumor cell."

19

Your Shadow Side—It is important to honor, understand, and be kind to all parts of ourselves. Shoving any parts of ourselves down inside and living in denial can be detrimental to our health.

Debbie Ford has some of the best books and DVDs on our shadow sides. *The Dark Side of the Light Chasers*, is one of her most popular. She has many others that are good including *Courage: Overcoming Fear and Igniting Self-Confidence.*

I remember one woman who was very proper and wore turtleneck sweaters, but she discovered that her shadow side preferred red slinky dresses. She was surprised and delighted to know that somewhere deep inside herself she was capable of such frivolity. She began to let her fun side out.

We tend to develop the side of us that gets all the positive pats on the back when we are children and growing up. The shadow side can be as innocent as an artistic side that is buried or it could be buried pain needing to be healed. We are such awesome, multifaceted beings that the journey to self discovery is like mining for diamonds. Diamonds do not sparkle when they are buried in muck.

20

Journal—Journaling is probably one of the simplest and least expensive healing tools around. However, it is not the easiest. It can be difficult to get people into the habit of journaling. It has been suggested that it takes twenty-one days to create a new habit. I highly recommend taking the twenty-one days to journal. If you put it on paper, it will not be hanging around in your body causing aches and pains. If you are worried about someone reading your journal, buy a lock box, hide it in your closet or under your mattress, or you can burn the pages or tear them up. It is well worth the effort. I also have clients who have had incredible results with drawing journals. I like small boxes of pastels because they really open one up creatively. One particular client said she could neither write nor draw. I explained that she had to do something for a physical release of her inner emotions. She finally agreed to do the drawing. Six months later she returned, not only as a happier woman but also as someone who had sold her first painting. It never ceases to amaze me what is locked up in our bodies.

Good sources are *Writing Down Your Soul: How to Activate and Listen to the Extraordinary Voice Within,* by Janet Conner and *Raw Art Journaling,* by Quinn McDonald and Tonia Davenport. Two others are *Artist Journal Workshop: Creating Your Life in Words and Pictures* by Cathy Johnson and *Journal to the Self: Twenty-Two Paths to Personal Growth-Open The Door to Self-Understanding by Writing, Reading, and Creating a Journal Of Your life* by Kathleen Adams.

"Learn to get in touch with the silence within yourself and know that everything in life has a purpose."—Elisabeth Kubler-Ross

21

Get a Massage—Massage is healing; it helps stimulate new red blood cells, calm the nervous system, and enhance circulation. Massage can also reconnect you to your body and reacquaint you with healthy touch. Take a class and make friends to exchange massages. Massage is a necessity, not a luxury. Research shows that massage can enhance most healing protocols by increasing endorphins. There is also evidence that massage can:

- slow the heart rate,
- lower blood pressure,
- relax muscles,
- increase blood circulation and lymph flow,
- improve range of motion,
- stimulate weak and inactive muscles,
- relieve stress,
- aid relaxation,
- alleviate discomfort during pregnancy,
- reduce formation of excessive scar tissue,
- reduce muscle spasms,
- enhance rehabilitation after injuries and operations,

- improve posture,
- enhance health,
- nourish the skin,
- promote deeper and easier breathing, and
- help relieve tension-related headaches and effects of eye-strain.

Some of the mental benefits of massage are that it fosters peace of mind, satisfies the need for caring, nurturing touch, reduces anxiety, enhances the capacity for calm thinking and creativity, and simply makes you feel good.

Research at the University of California in San Diego has shown that cancer protocols are much more effective with the added benefit of massage. I was impressed to find a list of massage benefits on the Mayo clinic web site.

Someday maybe insurance companies will see that it can save money to cover massage.

22

Movies—Go to movies with positive role models and inspiring true-life stories. *First Wives Club* came out during my divorce. It hurt to watch, yet it felt good that so many people understood the pain. *Under the Tuscan Sun* with Diane Lane is another movie with a good role model because her character creates a happy, new life for herself. You can get a box of tissues, your favorite movies, and let the tears flow. Many movies are a great escape from painful reality and provide much-needed laughter. You can rent movies and enjoy an emotional buffet in the privacy of your home.

Since I was a flight attendant for over twenty-five years and Paris was one of my favorite layover locations, *View from the Top* is special to me. This movie offers laughter and tears to soothe. Foreign films also soothe my soul. I love *The Story of the Weeping Camel*, which takes place in Mongolia. It is a beautiful story of healing and feelings.

The Himalayas is another delightful film about the beauty of people in others cultures. In this film a tribe completes a long held tradition for the last time. I love tradition, and it seems to me that many traditions are disappearing. Traditions hold people together from large to small groups. Getting together for a family dinner every evening and communicating doesn't happen as much these days.

My father insisted we had a family dinner together and the television had to be turned off. We always complained until we started eating and talking. We often sat at the table long after we were finished. Creating warm family traditions can get people through many of the stresses in life. Most families are now letting go of tradition in favor of the stresses. If you notice, families that fall apart don't seem to make time for a family dinner. The tradition of family dinner, game night, or movie night is important. I am soothed by French and British comedies as well as by great American comedies. Comedy films deserve more credit for their healing abilities. We usually do not associate laughter with social redeeming value. Laughter its-self is the gift. A family who laughs and cries together has a better chance of staying together.

Notice that movies without villains and/or challenges to overcome are boring and not as popular with moviegoers. If there is no villain or challenge, no one can change or grow and life is less interesting. Therefore, we accept our villains, challenges, and lessons that take us to growth, rewards, and a better quality of life. There is a lot to be gained by watching movies. I took a women's study class about women in movies. I learned so much that I would take it again.

23

Read—Today there are many books to help you move on and find healthy love. Spend time in the self-help section of your favorite bookstore or go online to amazon.com or barnesandnoble.com which both have great websites with book reviews and sometimes excerpts. When you find a book you like, the sites show other books purchased by people who bought the one you're interested in. I wanted to know what happened in my marriage so as not to make the same mistake again. It was time I learned not only about myself but also about women who could inspire me and make me proud to be a woman. I headed to my favorite bookstore and amazon.com.

I learned about women who took care of themselves in every way; like me, these women took life's lessons and learned how to balance their lives. I am a woman, and I need to respect women and respect myself. A book called *Mad Women* impressed me very much but I cannot find it anymore, I am sorry to say. I recommend reading *Women Who Run with the Wolves* by Clarissa Pinkola Estes. This book is best read with a highlighter. I also learned a lot from characters in novels. It is interesting to read about characters with similar circumstances coming through and surviving. It is healthy to read for pleasure and fun as well as for information.

Books by Louise Hay offer tools for self-exploration that start the healing process. Louise Hay, *You Can Heal Your Life* is my favorite. If you buy a great book that helps you, pass it on to another woman. As women begin to share instead of compete with each other, we will get stronger and healthier as individuals and as a group. I love bookstores and find great peace in a store filled with books.

> "In each of us are places where we have never gone. Only by pressing the limits do you ever find them."—Dr. Joyce Brothers

24

See Your Ex as a Teacher—Realize your ex is a teacher and list all that you learned from the relationship. My marriage was one *mean* university, but the knowledge is invaluable. Take time to assimilate everything you learned. Realize that this person came into your life for a reason, and that there are benefits from having had this relationship. Write letters to your ex, thanking him for the knowledge he helped you attain. I wrote many letters that I burned and never mailed. I am aware that I would not have such a wonderful, happy life now if I had not married and divorced that man. Finding gratitude will not be easy at first but the more you keep at it, the better you will feel. Release the negative and attract the positive into your life.

"Failure is success if we learn from it."—Malcolm Forbes

"Education: that which reveals to the wise
and conceals from the stupid the vast limits
of their knowledge."—Mark Twain

25

Being Right—Back when Dr. Phil was making guest appearances on Oprah, he made a statement I will never forget. He said he had given up doing couples counseling because rather than coming to him for advice; people came to be told they were right. Being right will not get you as far as just *being*. I now let almost everyone be right. The cost of being right is high. It can cost you friends, family, energy, peace of mind, and much more. I would rather be wrong and happy.

I am not advocating capitulation to avoid confrontations, however; it is important to know how to pick your battles. The difference is when you "need" to be right.

"No one can make you feel inferior without
your consent."—Eleanor Roosevelt

26

Ego—It is important to know what will compromise your ethics as this can wound the soul. It is also easy to get caught up with the ego. The ego can lead you on a path of self-destruction as it seeks satisfaction. You will learn to notice others who are driven by their egos and to avoid them. Notice when your ego is driving you, give yourself a hug, and let the situation go. In my work as a massage therapist, I know I can do more to help my clients if I tune into my work and keep my ego out. When I work on people I send my ego to have a cup of tea or sit outside. When I work on horses I send my ego to the car or a comfortable place outside. This makes me much more effective.

"Whenever I climb I am followed by a dog
called 'Ego'."—Friedrich Nietzsche

27

Choices—Life is filled with choices. Every day when we wake up, we have a choice to be happy or be miserable. We have a choice between being a person with ethics and being dishonest. We have a choice to live with honor or not. We have a choice to be true to our heart and soul or not.

I choose to be happy. I want to laugh a lot, and when I go to bed, I want to feel good about how I behaved as a human being during the day. I want to be proud of myself. I do not look for appreciation or accolades from anyone but myself. If I get them from others, I say "thank you." It is the icing on the cake. The only person I am concerned about pleasing is me. When I am happy with myself, all is well in the world.

"Once you make a decision, the Universe conspires to make it happen."—Ralph Waldo Emerson

"I don't know the key to success, but the key to failure is trying to please everybody."—Bill Cosby

# 28

The Gift—I was given the gift of life. It is up to me to show respect for that gift. I am grateful to be alive. I am enjoying my life experience and seeing myself survive. I see how strong and resilient I am, and this strength makes me realize I can do anything. I am looking forward to what I will do next.

Treat your gift of life with respect and watch how limitless you feel.

"You teach others how to treat you."—Dr. Phil

"You must understand the whole of life, not just
one little part of it, that is why you must read, that
is why you must look at skies, that is why you must
sing and dance, and write poems, and suffer, and
understand, for all that is life."—J. Krishnamurti

29

Intuition and Gut Feeling—I did not listen to my intuition when I first met my husband. If I had, I would never have gone out with him, let alone marry him. I also had a six-month rule that I abandoned. My gut instinct and my six-month rule would have saved me.

After seven and a half years with the wrong man, I blamed my instincts. I did not even trust myself to choose a book or a movie. Decision-making became very difficult. Some people believe in psychics, and some do not; I believe some are good and some are not. Every now and then, I like to see what they think, but I ultimately make up my own mind.

The day my husband moved out, I was feeling awful. He left the house a mess with half the household goods. I sat down alone to cry and feel sorry for myself. The television was on and I saw an ad for a psychic reading and thought *why not?* I was feeling totally lost and miserable. The psychic told me that if I were patient, then my husband would return. My crying turned to laughter as I realized the thought of him back in my life for one week, one day, or even one minute was completely unacceptable. I knew immediately that I was better off without him and that

I would create a new life for myself. That was the best money I spent at that time.

Alexandra of the Alexandra Institute in San Diego gave me unwavering support and was very positive. She reminded me that I was a strong woman and that I needed to learn to trust my own instincts again. She always assured me I would come out of the divorce like a phoenix raising from the ashes. Continuing to hold that picture in my mind helped me soar. My trust in myself and my own instincts strengthened every day. As I tell my clients, we must listen to our guts, temper it with our hearts, and use our heads to keep from falling off a cliff.

"Trust your hunches. They're usually based on facts filed away just below the conscious level."—Joyce Brothers

30

Pets—My dog Julie's role in saving me was huge and continued to make my life better until she passed away ten years after the divorce. She was also upset at the time, but we loved each other, and having her support was healing for me. We would take a daily three-mile walk through the neighborhood, chat with everyone along the way, and she would sit by me while I had coffee at the local café.

During my marriage, I was always working, trying to please my husband and avoid the truth. Divorce set me free; I had time to walk, think, read, do yoga, and all the things I suggest in this book. Best of all was spending time with Julie.

My dog continued to be my best friend, and our walks were the best part of my day. Not only was her love and support steadfast, but also she taught me a lot about love and asking for what you want. Pets help their owners have lower blood pressure and lower cholesterol levels (reducing the risk for heart disease), and pet owners get more exercise. They help against depression and loneliness, help children with self-esteem (since pets love them unconditionally and want their undivided attention), and elderly patients usually have fewer doctor visits. I hope Julie dog felt I gave her as much as she gave me.

Andrew Weil M.D. is one I admire for his well rounded study of eastern and western medicine. On his web site he has an article on Animal assisted therapy (AAT) which Dr. Weil states reportedly dates back to 1940, when an army corporal brought his Yorkshire terrier to a hospital to cheer wounded soldiers. There was such a positive response that the dog continued to comfort others for twelve more years. Pet Partners is a research based organization committed to promoting animal based treatment around the country. Dr. Weil's site mentions some of the health benefits that have been observed when animals comfort humans.

I have to tell you this story about Julie dog. When she found me she was between six and nine months old (she lived to be sixteen and a half years old) and walking would make her feet bleed. I used doggie socks and boots, but she did not like them. I knew there was a connection between the mind, body and soul and I believed that it worked with animals also therefore, I started kissing her feet and telling her how beautiful she was and how much I loved her. Her feet never bled again. The healing was immediate. Just a reminder that love heals! It is very interesting how fast animals make the connection. Recently I was doing massage on a client and just getting his shoulders relaxed and all of a sudden they were locked up and tight again. I stopped and said, "What are you thinking? You have just gone back to the way you were when you came in." He learned a valuable lesson and is smart enough to practice letting go of the worry that tightens his body.

Pets can give you a positive focus in life. I have a new best friend named Tara dog but Julie will always be one of the greatest loves and blessings of my life. I will probably have a dog until the day I die. They love nature as much as I do and are the greatest excuse for a walk.

"Animals are such agreeable friends—they ask no questions, they pass no criticisms."—George Elliot

"Love the animals. God has given the rudiments of thought and joy untroubled."—Fyodor Dostoyevsky

31

Pet Massage—Pet massage has been shown to lower your blood pressure, which in turn influences your immune system. As you build a bond with your pet, giving them a massage reminds you what safe love feels like and how we are connected to all of life. There is nothing like their sweet surrender and trust. We can learn a lot about love from our pets.

When I massage horses I feel as if I am taking a walk with God. Animals are so honest with their needs. The horses always tell me where to massage them and give me a thank you nudge before they tell me they are finished.

The greatest gift horses have given me is teaching me how to live in the moment. Since horses are prey animals, they must be sensitive to the moment or their lives could be in danger. As predators we tend to live in the past and future. I know that when I massage horses, I must be in the moment or I could be in danger. Interestingly, if I have a cold I can go do horse massage and just focusing on the present for a couple of hours will affect my immune system and get rid of the cold.

One day I decided to take a class on horse massage to pick up a few new techniques. Instead I witnessed women so insecure that they resulted to brutality. When the instructor punched a horse another student punched a horse. I was sick to my stomach. Because I was noticeably sickened, the instructor said I must be a "la la tree hugger." Indeed, I am. Growing up, my parents taught me respect for horses and nature. I have kissed and hugged trees and horses. I have worked with abused horses and they have learned that I will not hurt them but I will help them feel better and they love me. We have trust.

Shakespeare said, "A horse! A horse! My kingdom for a horse." I empathize with the feeling.

Being present with dogs also works, but since they are not a thousand pounds, we can ignore them easier and let our minds wander to the past and future. My dogs have always let me know exactly what they want and when. They ask for love when they need it, and they are not afraid to show love in return. We can learn a lot from animals.

There are many books on animal massage and I invite you to get one for your pet and learn how to relax and let go.

> "We can judge the heart of a man by his treatment of animals."—Immanual Kant

32

Walk—Walking is reported to be one of the best exercises for health. Studies show that walking can reduce the risk of coronary heart disease, enhance mental well-being, help reduce body fat, increase bone density, reduce the risk of some cancers, lower blood pressure, and promote flexibility and coordination.

I found myself during my walks. I feel walking helps with spirituality and can help those of us living in cement jungles get in touch with our nature as well as mother nature. Walking also provided a chance for me to meet my neighbors. One neighbor would serve me wine and snacks a couple of times a week, and another would dog sit if I had to go out of town. Another neighbor helped me find a new place to live when I had to move. My morning walks are a continuous prayer of gratitude for all the beauty in the world and in my life.

Dr. Mehmet Oz and Michael Roizen have a web page listing the benefits of walking which includes lowering your real age. Of course it is best to check with your doctor before adding any exercise.

> "Walking is man's best medicine."—
> Hippocrates (the father of medicine)

33

Music and Dance—Music can ease the pain. As a right brain activity, it can stimulate healing endorphins. Peaceful New Age music can soothe the nervous system and provide a creative environment. Some classical music will have the same effect, but you will need to experiment. Classical music can elicit emotions and help with healing if you are ready. Mozart refused to take credit for his music claiming it came from God. The music of Mozart is very healing and is most helpful for getting in touch with your inner feelings. If you do not want to deal with emotions, you might be better off playing New Age music.

I suggest finding positive songs that reinforce good feelings, such as "I Will Survive." I have always felt country music was therapeutic. You can cry in your beer or dance and shout. Spend time with your favorite music. Dance and release all the pain and negative emotion as you move about freely expressing yourself in movement. My generation loves the music from *The Big Chill* to work out feelings. It contains music for a myriad of emotions.

Currently I have Zumba and Wii Just Dance 4. I love them and they are great fun for the whole family to do together, with friends or alone.

Drums are probably one of the oldest musical instruments in existence. They were used to send messages, celebrate, and promote healing. Most cities have healing drumming classes with both African and Native American drumming styles. Fortunately, you do not have to know how to play drums to take a class and receive benefits from drumming. I have a set of conga drums and a Native American drum made by a Native American artist. My drums are among my most prized possessions. Drums are also a great meditation instrument.

Dancing is a great form of expression that can help with release of emotions. I love to play music from my generation and dance. Most cultures have one dance or more that brings the family and community together in joy. This also gets happy endorphins flowing through the body.

Music therapy is a degreed and credentialed profession that is the clinical and evidence based use of music interventions to aid individuals in accomplishing emotional and physical healing goals. I have taken a few classes and look forward to it becoming more wide spread. Music therapy is a gentle and lovely alternative therapy because not every therapy is for everyone.

"Music was my refuge. I could crawl into
the space between the notes and curl my
back to loneliness."—Maya Angelou

34

Write a Jingle—The right brain is connected to the parasympathetic nervous system. The healing endorphins it releases are calming and can relax muscles, lower blood pressure and aid digestion. Creating a positive jingle about yourself, who you are, and what you want can help bring your dreams to fruition. The right brain, the side of imagination and vision, is more powerful than the left brain, which handles speech; hence the saying, "talk is cheap." Sing it, see it, and it is yours. Singing is a simple tool with big results.

Singing and rhymes put you in touch with your heart and soul. Write it, sing it, and get a karaoke machine; let your voice ring out and you will feel your heart and soul heal. I have a few favorite singers I love to sing with while I am driving or in the shower. I used to say that if I were queen, I would make a law that everyone had to sing in the morning. I believe everyone would have a better day.

My heart loves to sing, and if I listen to its song, I can feel my body move into happiness.

35

Write Poetry—Many number one songs and some of the world's most-loved poetry were written in the depths of pain. Again, it puts your feelings on paper and out of your body and mind while easing mind chatter and facilitating good sleep. I love to write poetry and country lyrics. Once you allow the words and feelings to flow, you will surprise yourself. I wrote many poems for my healing, and I like reading them now to see how far I have come. I will never be a poet but I will always appreciate the art. Following is one of my poems.

Starving Woman
© 1997 Gay Lyn Fry

I sing you this song as a starving woman's last wish.
As I sing, she orders pizza pie and again fills up her dish.
This song is not about the death of a
body but the death of soul,
Death of instinct, creativity, humor,
all that makes a person whole.

When she was young, she was a beauty.
She lost her soul performing woman's duty.
For her hardest work in life, she got no wage.
But the wisdom she earned made her a sage.
Never taking time to hear her own story,
She feels like an old flag, tattered, faded glory.
Always taking care of others, always pleasing,
She could miss her finest hour, her best season.

In the early morning with no one else around,
She stares in the mirror disgusted by the pounds.
A tear rolls down her face. She feels empty inside.
She wishes she could find a place where she could hide.

Her soul is starving, so she orders pizza pie.
She eats and eats but still feels hungry. She wonders why.
No longer can she envision the pie in the sky.
She does not know why, so she eats a lemon pie.

To go naked in the world she is afraid.
Cannot remember the last time she laughed or played.
She prays but has forgotten how to listen.
Her eyes have lost their sparkle and their glisten.
Always told to work hard and strive for perfection,
She has suffered from a deep fear of rejection.
Locking her heart up in deep walls of steel
Robs her of hope to heal or feel.

36

Baths—Taking a bath is another thing we do not make time for, yet it can do so much for us. I not only took baths but also found time to use the hot tub. I believe water soothes the savage beast. I got in my hot tub first thing in the morning, last thing at night, and often a few times in between. My favorite time was the middle of the night. I would feel alive as I took in the sky, trees, and stars.

Bath time is a good time for aromatherapy. Put in a few drops of lavender oil, grapefruit oil, rosemary oil, or other favorite scent. Find a health food store in your area where they carry these fine products, and ask them to help you select one and explain how to use it.

My favorite bath mixture is to combine one cup of sea salt and one cup of apple cider vinegar. Sea salt will help pull out the pain while apple cider vinegar will help you feel light and squeaky-clean as well as balance the PH in your skin. Soak for at least twenty minutes. Learn how to grant yourself time and know you are worth it. Baths are very inexpensive medicine. I alternate, showering one day and taking a bath the next. I make sure I savor whichever one I am doing. I deserve to start my day richly.

I love to make my own bath salts and say a prayer over them. The prayer then surrounds me in the tub.

37

Plan for a Great Morning—I have a plan for a great morning for myself. This is my experience most days. I feel if this is my morning at least three days a week, then I am feeding my spirit. It goes like this:

1. Love on my puppy
2. Make bed and tidy room
3. Exercise and/or take a walk
4. Clean up from and feed puppy
5. Make coffee or tea
6. Look outside and say gratitude prayer
7. Shower or bathe and dress
8. Meditate
9. Take vitamins
10. Eat my yogurt and make calls
11. Toast or cereal and emails
12. See clients and/or visit mother
13. Ideally get lots of calls from publishers and future clients

I do not beat myself up if I do not do the whole plan. It is just a plan. My life is about me, not my plan. This is merely a guide of how I would like my day to look.

When you are sad or life is throwing you lessons faster than you can count them, it can be comforting to have a plan, be it as simple as a morning plan. The best part about keeping your life simple is that you do not set yourself up for failure. Many people set up grandiose plans that sound and look good but are too hard to do immediately. They fail and beat themselves up. They look at the failure as proof that they are losers. If we set up many simple plans that we can win, it will sustain us to go out and try the big stuff. When we go for the big stuff and fail we can fall back on all the little stuff where we have had success. We then have the strength to try more big stuff.

> "The one who follows the crowd will usually get no further than the crowd. The one who walks alone, is likely to find himself in places no one has ever been."—Albert Einstein

38

Nature—We get in touch with our own nature when we are *in* nature. Sitting in my hot tub, walking in the park, strolling on the beach, going on picnics, and camping kept me in touch with what is real and truly important in life. Divorce and courthouses are very unreal and unnatural. To keep sane, I would take a tent and my dog to a campsite in the mountains and spend the night. I would sit by the fire, look at the stars, listen to the sounds of nature, and walk in the woods. When I returned to the city the next day, I could see everything for what it was. I would then remember what really had value and what did not.

I strongly feel it is important to take a break from the urban lifestyle if you are to survive in the city. I remember one time when I needed to cry and could not get it out. I was alone so I went into my backyard, lay down on the grass, and requested, "Mother earth, please help me." I felt a warmth and tenderness surround me and tears began to flow.

I grew up in a beautiful rural town in Michigan. My parents taught me a great respect for and love of nature. I am so grateful for my beginning because I feel I was able to learn skills that have served me well.

I have moved back to my hometown and enjoy kayaking on the river, walking, and meditating by the lake. Did I mention trees? I love trees, especially pine trees. My aging mother and I would go for rides to look at and enjoy the trees. My mother has always had a special love of trees and has passed that on to me.

"To me a lush carpet of pine needles or
spongy grass is more welcome than the most
luxurious Persian rug."—Helen Keller

39

Faith—Faith is important to me. In the depths of pain, I cried out, "Jesus, Jesus, Jesus." Unfortunately, when all is going well, we do not think we need faith. In the last years of my marriage and during my divorce, I became *faith full*. My faith is important for minute-to-minute existence. I have also discovered Mary. Exploring Mary has led me to honor and respect the feminine in me and in the world. I believe in all that lives, and I believe in myself. Create your own positive prayer and write it out so you can read it often. Stick it on your bathroom mirror and put a copy in your purse or wallet. If you do not have a specific faith, feel free to create your own spiritual or faith-full practice.

> "I believe God is managing affairs and that He doesn't need any advice from me. With God in charge, I believe everything will work out for the best in the end."—Henry Ford

The Labyrinth and Meditation—It is in the stillness that we find our spirit, our spirituality, and ourselves. "Be still and know that I am God" (Psalm 46:10). Calming the mind and stilling the chatter help us make clear decisions and create peaceful, happy days. Our senses are bombarded every minute with thousands of bits of information, most of which are useless. Therefore, we must remember to give our minds time to clear. Take a class on meditation or join a group if you have difficulty in the beginning. You can learn meditation on your own; it just takes practice. The benefits to your health and well-being will become evident very quickly.

I discovered the benefits of a labyrinth, a medieval tool for balancing the mind and body. Labyrinths were created prior to the Spanish Inquisition and are often used for walking meditation or prayer. Some think labyrinths were designed to rebirth humankind, among other things. The labyrinth transforms and transmutes. I walked the labyrinth in the cathedral in Chartres, France, and it changed my life. I was inspired to purchase a canvas labyrinth and give labyrinth classes in San Diego. As a member of the First United Methodist Church Labyrinth group I had the privilege of facilitating many walks for groups of all ages, religions and positions in life. It was a joy for me to train as a facilitator with the Reverend Lauren Artress of Grace Cathedral in San Francisco. You can find more information in Reverend Artress's book, *Walking a Sacred Path: Rediscovering the Labyrinth as a Spiritual Tool.*

An added benefit to meditation and walking a labyrinth is the stimulation to the parasympathetic nervous system, which, as I mentioned before, calms the body. When the body is calm it can begin to heal itself.

Deepak Chopra offers a twenty-one day meditation challenge on his website free from time to time; the changes I have experienced from doing this challenge have made me a believer in the power of meditation. I know I must make time for it. Try it and you will wonder why you did not do it sooner.

41

Candles—Candles are a great tool to help you learn how to focus and meditate. I have heard that some businessmen in London leave a candle burning on their desks to maintain a calm atmosphere. I have also found candles burning in some American business offices. I almost always have candles burning. I make sure they are in safe containers in case I forget about them. Candles not only create a feeling of serenity, but they can also be a reminder to let the light within you shine.

Let Your Light Shine Meditation

Make yourself comfortable in a quiet place where you will not be disturbed. Close your eyes, and with your eyes closed look up, and then look straight ahead. Take three long, slow deep breaths taking the breath all the way down to the navel, filling up the chest, and holding for just a second before gently letting the breath go. Let your whole body relax. Relax your shoulders and all the way down your body to the tips of your toes. Relax your face. Relax your eyes and all around your mouth including your jaw. Take your awareness to your heart. Imagine there is a little door and you can step into your heart. Look for the little light. Notice what color it is and then step into this light. Notice how it feels. As you enjoy the feeling, let the light fill up your heart and then begin to fill your whole body. Let the light fill every cell of your body from the top of your head to the tips of your toes. Let your body feel so full that the light begins to shine from inside out through the pores of your skin, creating an aura of light all around you. Keep this feeling inside you and keep your body full of this light as go about your days and nights. Be aware of letting your light shine. Keeping your body full of your light, slowly bring yourself back to your room. Go about your life in light and love.

42

Exercise—Exercise not only for weight loss but also to feel good. If you get to a more desirable weight, that is an added bonus. Feeling good is your first priority, so let the endorphins flow. Yoga, tai chi, and chi-gung are particularly good because they will help you reconnect with your body and whole being. They will also help you breathe. Most people do not breathe correctly or deeply enough. Learn to breathe long, deep breaths all the way down to your navel. When we are under stress, we do not breathe deeply enough, and the oxygen is shut off to our bodies. Our bodies then become too stressed to operate. We set ourselves up for a very strong stress cycle. Yoga, tai chi, and chi-gung will help you develop your inner and outer strength.

I taught yoga during my marriage and divorce. I give it credit for much of my tranquility. Yoga is a great way to start the day and the rest of your new life. It is interesting to note that all other creatures on earth stretch. Babies and animals stretch but adult humans do not usually take the time to do it. Stretching enhances your circulation, and improves flexibility and mobility. Yoga helps me to be free of aches and pain. You deserve the time it takes to stretch; your body and mind will feel much better.

43

Naked—Spending one hour naked in front of the mirror is a great way to become reacquainted with yourself. Sit alone in your nakedness and journal what you are feeling. Notice if you are overly critical. Look for the positive. Your first goal is to make friends with yourself; this friend needs to feel safe, appreciated, and loved by you. You must practice being gentle and kind to yourself. Set the standard for how you want others to treat you.

I took a creative writing class at Johns Hopkins University, and the instructor said, "If you want to be a writer, you have to be able to go naked in the world." At that time I got indignant and thought I was just going to write with my imagination. Since then I have learned that she was correct. In fact, I believe you need to be able to go naked in the world to be healthy. While writing this book I am so happy to be naked and expose myself. It feels so freeing.

"The body says what words cannot."—Martha Graham

44

Change your Style and Hair—Changing your hairstyle sounds simple, and you may feel like you cannot take one more change. However, just parting your hair differently, changing the color, adding highlights, or changing the length can affect how you feel about yourself. Add different colors to your wardrobe. Change your style of clothing or dress. Remember, it is about taking charge and feeling good about yourself. Now is a great time to recreate yourself and let the real you shine.

Feeling free and beginning to express myself, I began to experiment with hair color; I colored my hair darker brown, then black, then even red. At present I am blonde and having lots of fun. I must say, I never in my life thought I would be a blonde, but I am loving it. I learned I am more than the color of my hair, what I wear, where I live, or being a wife.

45

Dine Out—If you can, eat out in a restaurant where a woman dining alone is treated like royalty. I found a Chinese restaurant near me that steamed fresh vegetables and treated me like family. It was a comfortable, safe place for me to be with others and also enjoy being with myself.

A coffee shop where everyone knows your name is also a great start to building a new world around you. Make sure it is a place where *you* are known, not your ex. I love taking myself out to dinner or lunch and trying new places.

46

Flowers—Flowers always make me feel special. They make a beautiful treat to oneself. Potted plants are nice because they last longer. Gardening and putting your hands in dirt is also very therapeutic. I like to grow things from seeds. I have two apple trees that I grew from the seeds of my favorite apple. It represents a new life, a new beginning, and hope for the future. I have nine strawberry plants. They don't provide enough strawberries for a feast, but they do give me a sweet treat. Almost every day I can eat one. I also have fresh mint for my tea and a lemon plant to season my cooking. Read *The Secret Life of Plants* for an interesting treat.

"The earth laughs in flowers."—Ralph Waldo Emerson

47

Take Yourself on a Date—I love taking myself on dates. I can go to a play or movie and not worry if it appeals to anyone else. I can spend as much time in a bookstore as I like without someone pacing outside. I can eat my favorite food, go for an extraordinary dessert, or walk and window-shop at a mall. It is fun to take in sights normally reserved for tourists. Use your imagination and create fun dates for yourself. Have fun and be free. Enjoy your own company. I love being with myself because I do not shut me down. I allow myself to be open and free. I am a great date for myself.

48

Take a Class—Classes in pottery, computers, painting, financial planning, or even basket weaving can help you meet new people and expand your horizons. Try dancing, a foreign language, piano, golf, tennis or guitar. My last class was astronomy, and I love knowing a little more about the universe. Many classes will give you valuable tools as well as the opportunity to meet people with similar interests.

I took a sailing class and found early mornings on the ocean so calming that I believed I could handle anything after a morning sail. I used to put a lifejacket on my dog and take her with me. Near where I lived, a couple of large hotels on the ocean rented small sailboats. It was beautiful, so I was surprised that Julie dog and I were the only ones on the ocean in the morning.

At my local college in Alpena I took a class is astronomy which I recommend because it does help us to put ourselves in prospective. I have always said that I could not let someone who occupies such a small amount of molecules in the whole scheme of things affect my life for the negative. Now I have discovered on the NASA web site that with the equipment today (New cameras and telescopes are created everyday) over 100 billion galaxies are visible. We live in the Milky Way Galaxy. Think about it...over 100 billion are visible. It boggles the mind. I feel like a grain of sand.

49

Photography—Taking pictures has always given me so much pleasure. I take thousands of pictures a year now, thanks to my digital camera. You will rarely see me without my camera. I love to catch sunrises and sunsets on the river where I grew up. When I go out in my kayak, I always have my camera and keep trying to get a different look at the same thing.

While in Australia assisting a client with the birth of her second child, I visited the Melbourne Zoo and got the best picture of a butterfly. I love looking for things to shoot in nature. When my father was alive he used to love to take my niece and me for rides in the country to find barns, trees, ponds, deer, and other awesome sites in nature. He was always patient as I trekked around trying to get the perfect shot. The best gift of any class you take is a new view of your surroundings and life.

Working with a camera can help you to get a new and closer look at the world around you.

"Anyone who keeps the ability to see beauty
never grows old."—Franz Kafka

50

Take a Trip—Getting out of town can always help you get a fresh look on a stale situations. Go where no one will ask about your ex. I took a class in France that changed my life. I was able to release many layers by walking the labyrinth in Chartres Cathedral. The good thing about getting away is that when you come home you can look at your situation more objectively.

I have had the pleasure of having a travel filled life and again I think one of the biggest lessons is that nothing is as big as you think it is. The world is huge and if you go to the Worldometers real time world statistics web site you will see that there are about 7 billion people on this planet. There is just more in the world then an issue with one person. I believe it is important to look at the big picture from time to time.

51

Write the Story of Your Life—Writing down the story of your life can help you see who you are and how you got there. Looking at our history can help us see the patterns in our lives. Many times the awareness alone can help us break old habits and trends. Start with a timeline chart of major events in your life and then fill in between those events. You can then see the patterns you have created. We keep repeating until we experience the straw that breaks the camel's back; then we have a chance to break the pattern and create a new life.

> "There is no greater agony than bearing an untold story inside you."—Maya Angelou

52

Your Hands—Do things with your hands. I love to watch people's hands and how they use them. My neighbor's hands on a piece of wood are breathtaking. I love the way my hands look on a body when I'm giving a massage. My hands seek out pains on a body and I trust them. They find areas that my mind does not find. Watch a good seamstress with hands on fabric. Watch a kind nurse put her hands on a patient. Notice how a baby responds to its mother's hands and how a pet lover strokes his or her pet. Refinish a piece of furniture, make some jewelry, or take a class in sculpture. Enjoy the gifts your hands can create. I feel I put love into all I do with my hands.

In yoga we learn that holding your hands in prayer position at your heart center calms your body.

> "The Hand is the visible part of the brain."—Immanuel Kant

53

Career—Look at your career. How does it make you feel about yourself? If it is time for a change, what will it take? Start planning now. You will do well to change, especially if you work at the same place as your ex. Update your resume, talk to some job placement agencies, and put yourself out there. It could be time to start the career of your dreams.

I love putting myself out there and enjoying whatever the universe brings me.

"Don't make money your goal. Instead, pursue the things you love doing and do them so well that people can't take their eyes off you. All the other tangible rewards will come as a result."—Maya Angelou

54

Poster—Make a poster using pictures and words from magazines. Make the poster about what you want for your life. Put the poster somewhere where you can see it often. When you know what you want, you have a better chance of obtaining it. I have used this technique with many people, including myself; everyone is always surprised when the poster becomes reality.

I do a new poster at least once a year. I like to do one for the New Year. I often get a group of family and friends together for this powerful annual event. We have fun gathering magazines that will have pictures and words that are part of our dreams. Oprah's magazine is great for making posters. Feel free to add to your poster all year long. My life very much resembles the pictures on my poster. I am creating the life of my dreams.

55

Truths and Fears—It is important to look at your truths. What is true for you and about you? You can keep this list of truths in your journal, in a separate notebook, in your purse, or by your bed. You will surprise yourself as you get to your core beliefs. The truth is, my marriage was over before it began. Everything I feared about marriage came true. We often attract what we fear. I am now very aware of my truths and fears. Clearing your fears clears the path for a happy life.

Often, just the awareness can help you let them go or lighten their effect on your life.

"I can be changed by what happens to me, but I refuse to be reduced by it."—Maya Angelou

56

Honesty—Being honest with yourself is one of the greatest gifts you can give yourself. You will attract someone who is where you are. If you want a good friend you will need to be one to yourself. I like making a list of lies that I used to believe about me and my life. I started the list, and I add to it periodically as I become aware of them. My deeply held misconceptions were all a mystery to me. It has taken work to bring them to my consciousness. I do not want to live a lie. I want to live in truth and authenticity. It does not happen overnight. It takes work, but it is rewarding work. I applaud myself with each new discovery I make about myself. I am working on myself to become the person I want to attract in my life.

> "If you want the truth, I'll tell you the truth: Listen to the secret sound, the real sound, which is inside you."—Kabir

57

Stay positive—Keep a gratitude journal and put positive sayings on your bathroom mirror and refrigerator. Louise Hay has a set of "Power Thought" cards that are a great tool. You can also create cards of your own with your favorite positive sayings from books, poetry, movies, or friends. I like to draw one each day and keep that thought in my mind as I go about the day. When you encounter negative people, excuse yourself. Protect yourself and stay positive. Happiness is a choice. You can choose happiness for yourself. I say "Thank you, God" all day long when I see something beautiful, enjoy a moment of life, or just feel grateful for all that surrounds me. My life is a continuous prayer of gratitude.

I especially ask new mothers to make an excuse to leave when they encounter people who want to share a horrendous experience they or a friend had. It is important to know you can have a good experience. Someone else's experience is not your experience.

> "When I look at the future, it's so bright,
> it burns my eyes."—Oprah Winfrey

58

Play and Laugh a Lot—Watch funny movies or go to a comedy club. Television shows like *Ellen, Everybody Loves Raymond, Friends, America's Funniest Home Videos, The Planet's Funniest Animals, The Big Bang Theory,* and many more. Laughter heals! When you make the sound, "Ha, ha, ha" (even if you fake it) it resonates in the belly and causes your body to release healing endorphins. Norman Cousins feels he cured himself of an "incurable illness" with laughter. He now has a clinic and research center to help others do the same.

Play with children or play like a child. Go to a theme park. Laughter and play will rejuvenate your heart and soul. Experience life as Tom Hanks does in the movie *Big.* He truly found the heart of a child as he acted the part. I've purchased a box seat at the circus for myself and bought candy and toys for myself. I've played the child. You can fake laughter and it will still have healing benefits. Therefore, with laughter it pays to fake it until you make it.

I will never forget the feeling when I heard my own laughter for the first time in a long time after I was separated from my husband. I then made a promise to myself that

I would create a life with laughter for my precious self. If I have to rent funny movies, standup comedian DVDs, or call my cousin Pam to laugh, I will. I have found there are some people with whom you laugh a lot when you get together. When I go kayaking with my delightful cousin Pam we run into each other; I can't help but laugh because even with a whole river we still run into each other. She is such a joy.

"Even the Gods love jokes."—Plato

"Hearty laughter is a good way to jog internally without having to go outdoors."—Norman Cousins

59

Write Letters Not to be Mailed—Writing letters is a great way to let go of people who are either still living or have passed on. Some people like to mail the letters they write if the person is living. For me, it is enough to write the letters and read them aloud to myself or to a close friend. You will have to decide what is best for you. I also like to write letters and burn them. I love this technique for letters to parents as well as to loved ones. A boss, neighbor, coworker, or in-law who makes you a little nuts is a good prospect. Writing letters helps me see the situation for what it is. Then I can see my role in the drama, see why the other person and I have a conflict, and peacefully let it go. This really works for me.

60

Go For a Drive—Go for a drive in the country and focus on the view, or just drive to an area of town that you have not been to before. While in San Diego, I would go for a ride to find my dream house. I would choose different areas each time and enjoy the beautiful homes. Whether they were seaside, bluff side, or in the desert or mountains, the homes were all so beautiful and would have provided different life styles. Exploring a new shopping mall, flea market, or farmers' market can also add adventure to your life.

In Michigan I go for a drive to count deer and look for eagles or other critters. My hometown has pretty streets as well as lush country side. Remember, it is all about exploring life and finding new reasons to be alive. There is so much more to life than a bad relationship.

"Come forth into the light of things, let nature be your teacher."—William Wordsworth

My beautiful and lively mother swinging on a swing she built.
She climbed the tree and hung the rope. Her age here is 83.

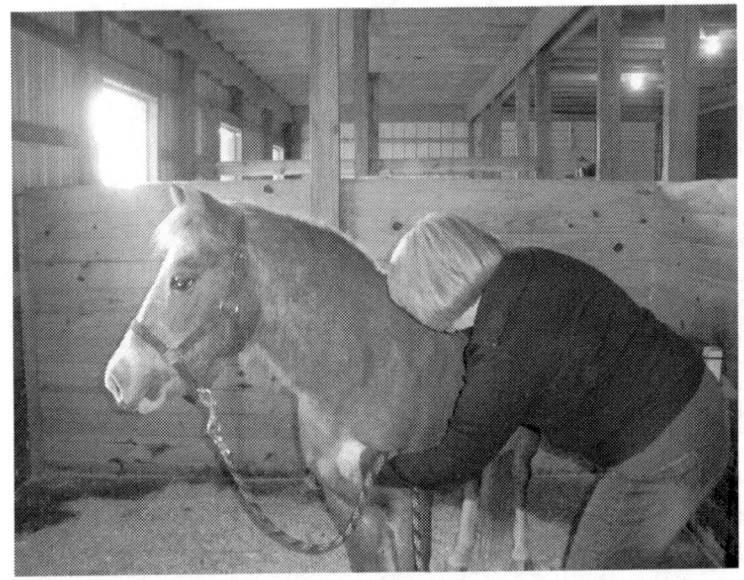

Trixie had been abused and did not like being touched. She loves massage and will makes sure she gets hers. She will stand in an open stall, free to leave, and get her massage.

Going for a kayak ride with Tara dog. Life is good.

Liberty was abused by trainers who wanted to control
her. She just wanted to survive. She loves massage
and always shows her gratitude with a hug.

A water lily on the river I love.

I am riding a camel named Moses in Egypt.

The famous Shakespeare and Company Bookstore is located across from Notre Dame in Paris, France. The owner since 1951, George Whitman is in the background and would allow want-to-be writers to sleep among the books for free.

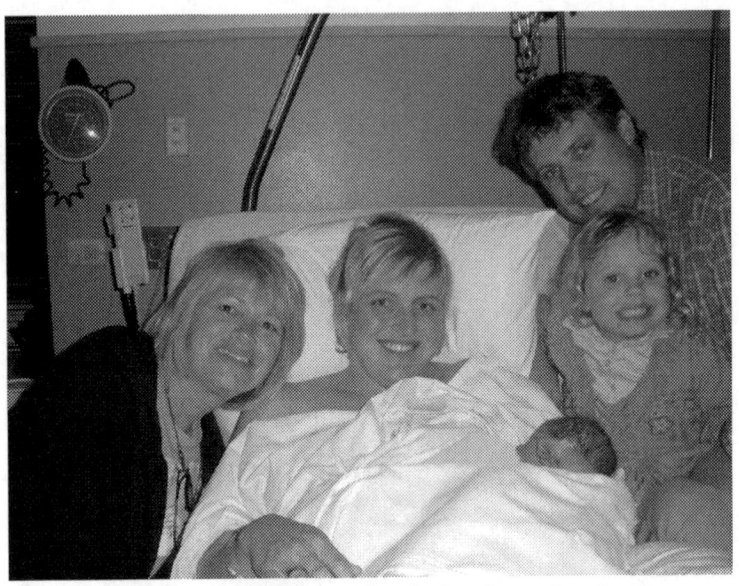

I had the honor to be the Doula for the Bailey family
twice. The first birth for parents Leanne and Michael
was little girl Aibhlinn in San Diego, Ca. and the second
was little boy Eoghan in Melbourne, Australia.

I had the honor of officiating at the wedding of Stacie and
Jim Johnston at the Boyne Highlands Resort in Michigan.

Walking on the beach in San Diego, California
with my beautiful Julie dog.

Preparing to teach a yoga teacher certification class.

I love this river and its many beautiful views.

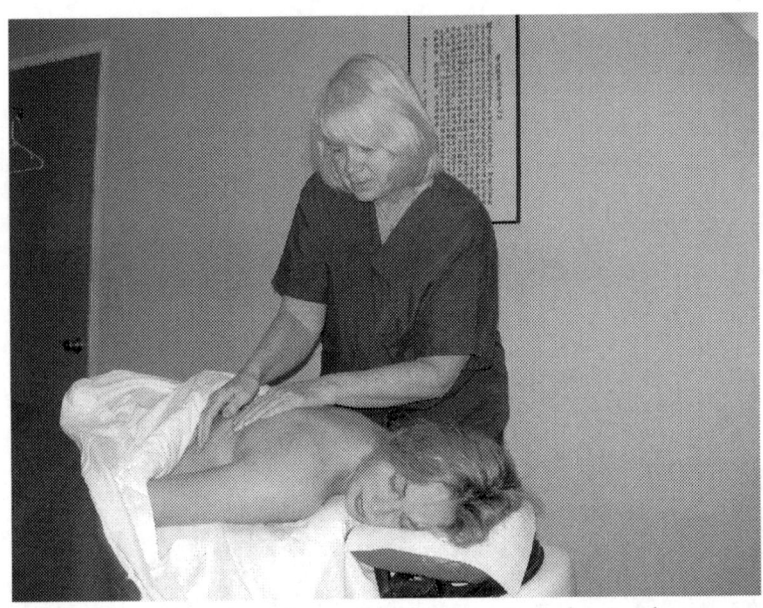

I am blessed to give massage to people and animals.

A small peek at the harbor of my picturesque home
town of Alpena, Michigan on Lake Huron.

I am kayaking on my beloved river. Notice the
feather lightly resting on the water.

I walked to the center of the labyrinth at *Garden of Healing and Renewal*, McLaren Health Care Village in Clarkston, Michigan

Gypsy is one of the most loving and lovable beings. She is patient and forgiving of me for being a horrible rider.

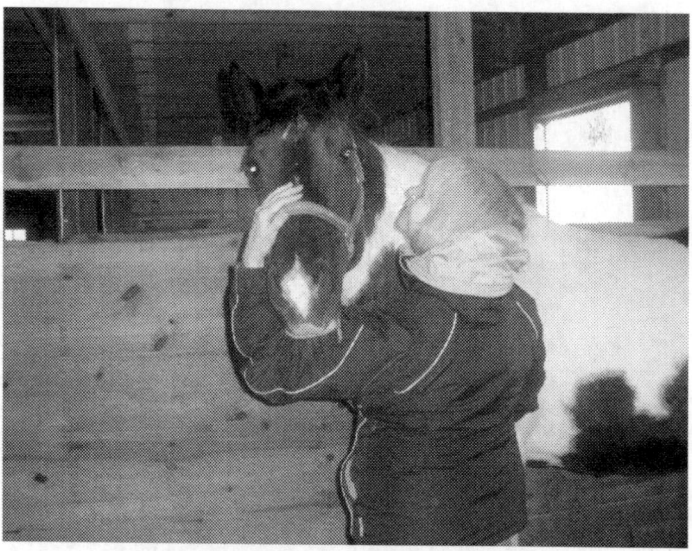

Margarita gives me a hug. I love horse hugs. Horses are not afraid to show appreciation.

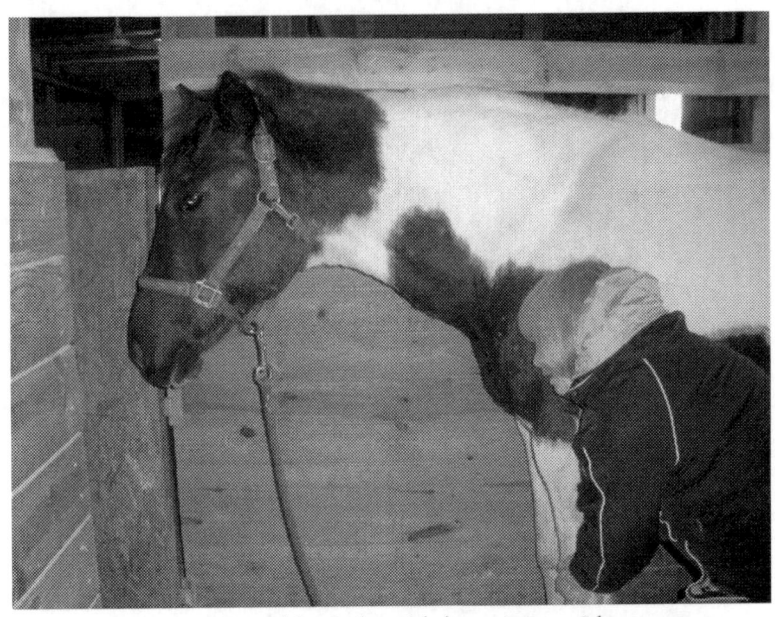

Margarita is an older lady with knee issues. I hope you can see her glazed eyes and notice her stall is open.

My cousin Pam Ruth and I hug the peace tree at *Garden of Healing and Renewal*.

I had the honor of officiating at the wedding of Melodi and Ryan Suszek on the beach in Rogers City, Michigan. I am blessed to attend special moments in people's lives.

61

Breathe in Life—Yogis and alternative health practitioners have known for a long time that conscious breathing can help reduce stress, increase relaxation, and reduce pain. We are born breathing correctly, but life's happenings, events, and growing pains cause us to clench our teeth, bring our shoulders up near our ears, and breathe shallowly. We need the oxygen from breathing to stimulate proper blood circulation to all the vital organs. When the body gets the oxygen it needs, it is calm and peaceful. Long, slow deep breaths reduce pain, stress, and depression. They also improve overall well-being and increase one's life span. The shortest-lived animals are those which breathe rapidly. The longest-lived animals are the ones take slower breaths.

I have had the pleasure of attending a lecture with famed neuroscientist Candace Pert, Ph.D. Her book, *Molecules of Emotion*, tells us that bringing our attention to our breathing during meditation gives us numerous health benefits. I always tell my clients that you can change your life by following your breathing three minutes a day. But I have heard others say to start with just one minute. You will feel so remarkably better that you will increase the time you spend with yourself breathing.

Most people do not breathe correctly. When you inhale, your body needs to expand and fill with oxygen, and as you exhale your body relaxes and contracts to expel the stale, old air. It is important to inhale into your diaphragm and lungs. Many people only breathe into one of these organs.

Dr. Andrew Weil has CD's to help teach you breathing techniques to enhance your health and give you peace of mind.

Having trouble sleeping? Spend some time breathing long, slow deep breaths and you will most likely sleep like a baby.

62

Cooking—Cooking for yourself, cutting vegetables, and putting love into your food is healing. Choosing your veggies, looking at the color, and putting your precious time into your nourishment are all important. The time and effort you put into the food that fuels your body communicates how you care for yourself. I took a class from a gourmet vegetarian cook in San Diego who taught how important it is to make your kitchen peaceful. He also stressed the importance of knowing that how you feel when you cook comes across in your food. Have you eaten food made by someone who loves to cook? It is awesome because you can feel their joy of cooking. That joy is healing. When you cook for yourself or your family or friends, let your love flow from your hands to the food.

"I have made a lot of mistakes falling in love, and regretted most of them, but never the potatoes that went with them," –Nora Ephron

63

A Healthy Diet—selecting healthy foods and making healthy food choices is again giving your body quality fuel for a healthy mind and nervous system. I also love vitamins. I watch Dr. Oz, and I respect and listen to him because he continues to learn and gets so excited when he has new information on the benefits of a herb. He recommends taking a multi-vitamin, vitamin D3, and fish oil each day. You can add other vitamins as you feel the need or gain more information and knowledge of your body and what it needs.

What you feed your body tells it how you feel about your gift of life. Your body is a living organism. Feed it with love, care and healthy choices.

Set yourself up with a healthy plan that you can put into action. Do not set yourself up for failure. Create a gentle, feasible plan. Remember, do not create such a strong regimen that you cannot do it and therefore abandon it.

Information on foods, vitamins, and new products changes every day. It is necessary to keep informed for our health just as we would for fashion, cars, games, new trends, or other information that is important to us.

64

Gardening—Plant a small garden and eat what you grow. Tomatoes, radishes, and carrots are just a few foods you could grow, eat, and feel good about yourself as you nourish your body. I love going for a walk in the yard and eating my own strawberries. When I lived in California I had an avocado tree and enjoyed taking care of the tree and gaining the benefits of its fruit. One of the first things I planted in Michigan was strawberries. I love going out and eating a few strawberries that I grew myself.

Radishes are important to me because I love radish sandwiches. The flavor of home-grown radishes is so special to me because for many years my grandfather would grow radishes just for when I came home to visit. My grandfather also had the best apples.

Putting your hands in the dirt, watering, and caring for plants can be healing. In the room where I write I have large plants. My entryway has plants and I cannot have a kitchen without plants. Plants make the air I breathe so fresh.

"In search of my mother's garden, I found my own."—Alice Walker

65

Make a List of Things You Have Never Had Time to Do and Begin!—It is never too late to explore your adventurous side. This could mean trying calamari at a restaurant by the sea, trying on clothes at Saks, or wandering through art galleries. I love art galleries. I have learned a lot by wandering through a few galleries time after time. I will take classes until I am too old to get to them. I work to make time for them. Much of it is about saying, "I have all the time in the world." I have all the time in the world, and I intend to spend it with passion."

"Time is what we want most, but what
we use worst."—William Penn

66

Make a List of What You Want in a Relationship—I have a little book with lists of what I want in a relationship, as well as goals, hopes, and desires for my life. I am always adding to my list of qualities that a good mate would have. I am aware that I must also have these qualities. I'd like my mate to be honest, have integrity, not take himself seriously, have a great sense of humor, be a healthy eater, love dogs, love nature, be interested in wind and solar power, love Paris, love to travel, love to kayak, love to walk, be adventurous ...and on and on the list goes. Knowing what your deal breakers are and when to compromise is where the pondering comes in.

67

Make a List of People Who Put a Wet Blanket on Your Ideas—Become aware of those who could dampen your spirits and goals. Avoid them like the plague. It is called taking care of yourself and protecting your spirit. Everything is about awareness. If you are aware of your hopes, desires, and dreams, and are also aware of those who could put out your fire and passion, you are halfway there. I have an acquaintance who has never said, "Good for you," "Good job," or anything close to telling me I was okay. Whenever I do well or accomplish something she gets a sad look on her face. For awhile I downplayed all I did and got negative about myself to keep her happy. I refuse to do that anymore. I continue to tell her, "Good job" and give her an "atta girl," but I do not expect anything in return and I limit my exposure to her.

It is important to have people in your life who are happy for you when you succeed. A good friend is one who maximizes your successes and minimizes your failures. A good friend does not tell you what to do, but instead listens as you figure it out for yourself.

Remember; do not diminish your light for anyone. Let your light shine.

> "As we let our light shine, we unconsciously give other people permission to do the same. As we are liberated from our own fear, our presence actually liberates others."—Marianne Williamson

68

Vampires—Vampires in real life can be just as handsome, charming, and seductive as those in the movies. They are very clever and can seduce the smartest of people. I am amazed at how many very smart men and women are seduced by vampires. Most vampires want only the best. They will look for the smartest and richest because they want all you have. Those rich in energy, creativity, connections, money, or charm are targets because they are always looking for what can benefit them. They want someone with a lot to offer because they intend to suck it all up and leave you dry. They then move on to another victim. Be aware because they are not always easy to spot. When you notice that your life is all about feeding them and their needs, it is often too late. Check your energy level and notice what or who is depleting you.

69

Who Am I—"Who am I" is one of the best exercises I experienced at the Chopra Center when I was going through my divorce. Make a list of who you are and who you are not. Always be willing to change your list. Close your eyes, sit back, relax, ask the question, and savor the answers. Ask yourself this question often. Deepak Chopra would probably have you focus on this question for weeks. As someone who has done this exercise, I can tell you it is powerful.

This may seem like a simple exercise but do not ignore it. I have had many an enlightening experience with this exercise. It will change who you think you are and help you see who you really are.

70

Puzzles— Keep puzzles handy to keep your mind active and not on your ex. Reading books and doing puzzles can help keep your mind off your ex, as can practicing meditation and visualization, You can keep books or puzzles nearby or in your purse to have them handy. Dwelling on who he was, what he did, what could have been, or what you should have done are all exercises in futility. Let it go, and keep your mind on your new life. Many people find it hard not to think about their exes every minute of the day. The 111 steps in this book are important because they will help get this person off your mind and get your mind on yourself. You are the most important person in your world. Therefore, your most important job is to get yourself together and bring yourself to wholeness. You will then be ready to have a healthy relationship with another whole person.

71

Create New Habits—Change your old habits to fresh, new ones that help you realize you have a new life. Change the time you get up and the time you go to bed. Change what you eat, where you eat, what shows you watch on television, and the books you read. Do not let your life order you around; take charge! You will begin feeling empowered instead of feeling like a victim. Be aware of making everything your choice. I like to break up my routine with new choices.

"The Unfortunate thing about this world is
that good habits are so much easier to give up
than bad ones."—Somerset Maugham

72

Volunteer—Volunteering your time and service not only helps others but also can heal you in numerous ways. You either see life experiences as being beautiful and you are inspired, or you see that you have it much better than you thought. Either way, you win, and so does someone else. Giving to your community can show you that there is so much more to life than one person. I volunteered as a doula (someone who nurtures women during labor and delivery) at a major medical facility. My work of mothering new moms as they were about to give birth, watching husbands fall in love with them all over again, and witnessing a new life being born made me feel like the richest woman in the world.

Most towns have a list of places where you can volunteer. Giving and sharing what you have or who you are will light up the world as well as your soul.

> "It is one of the most beautiful compensations of this life that no man can sincerely try to help another without helping himself."—Ralph Waldo Emerson

73

Couple Role Models—I don't think we have very many positive role models as far as couples go. Most novels, movies, sitcoms, and even dinner discussions are about problems couples are having. My parents never fought in front of us, so I had no idea how to disagree. I did not know how to be myself and still be part of a couple. I have since learned there is no magic to a healthy relationship other than two emotionally healthy people. Learn how to be yourself and find someone who respects you as you respect them for who they are. It is important to think about what kind of relationship you want before getting married or moving in together; look realistically at how you complement each other. Can you both continue to grow in the relationship? Both of you must be able to grow, not just one of you. The key is to always remember why you fell in love and to continue to appreciate your partner for those traits. Expecting them to change is heading for disaster.

The old television show, *Mad About You*, is the only show I know of that gives a good example of a married relationship. Good relationships don't usually make entertainment. This show is now in reruns.

74

Find Your Voice—Many women shut down their voices in a relationship. Reclaiming your voice and learning how to use it are both important in your quest for wholeness. This is probably one of the hardest of all the steps but will take you nearest to your goals. It is important to note that you will overuse your voice and underutilize it before you find the correct balance. Note to self: always retain the power of your voice. I have always felt that my voice had the mute button on. My brother used to have music playing and the television was on in the background with the mute button on. I find I put my mute button on when in a conflict. My goal is to live with my mute button off.

As I look back at how I was raised, I see that I was supposed to be a "lady." The message I got was that ladies are just supposed to smile. They never say what they really think or feel. That is why so many young girls got molested. No one talked about it, so the perpetrators were free to pick and choose their targets. Also, people were told that babies and children don't remember what happened to them, so perpetrators were set free to molest more children. Now we have a world of hurt, abused adults who are choking on their pain and secrets.

As a Doula, I have watched molested and abused women struggle to have a baby when all the fear inside them tells them to keep their legs together. If they tell me ahead of time, often I can help them. Once I worked with a beautiful new mother who did not remember being molested. She did not remember but she still suffered the results. The midwife, doctor, nurse, and I suspected something had happened to her because she would not let the baby out. During her struggle, she told us she also had trouble with sex. The staff and I then knew for sure.

At one point the woman's mother and I were in the hall. She told me she wondered if having been molested when she was three could have had an impact on her daughter's failure to progress. She then explained that her family doctor at that time told her not to tell the child because she would not remember.

I could go on and on with stories of abused women and men who, when I helped them feel safe, began to tell stories they had kept inside. These crimes against children know no boundaries. Thanks to my heroine, Oprah, people now feel safer talking about it and even fight against abuse and molestation. I feel that prior to Oprah, the mute button was on.

75

Guilt and Shame—Guilt and shame are about the divorce being your fault and having the feeling that something is wrong with you. Guilt and shame are killers. They kill your spirit and shut you down. Some take in guilt and shame, while others dish it up. In any case, it is important to accept responsibility for your part, but to not take it on like a heavy burden.

Beware of those who make you feel guilty for their unhappiness.

"If you cannot find peace within yourself, you will never find it anywhere else."—Marvin Gaye

76

Forgiveness—Forgiveness is probably one of the hardest parts of any relationship, including the one with yourself. It is important to remember that you are not saying that any behavior is okay. You are just saying *I am letting it go so I can be free to live and grow.* Setting yourself free to live and grow is all forgiveness means. I found it easier to forgive my ex than the judge in our divorce. First, I made a list of all the people who made me angry and who played a part in all the deception. There were many people involved in the whole ugly scenario, including myself. I always look at people's history, and I see where they learned their behavior. I could not let go immediately, but my intention to let go was my guide.

The judge was another issue, however. I saw my ex as a problem to himself so I could let him go. The judge was sitting up there with power over my life and others' lives. He was supposed to keep his personal issues at home. In my opinion, he brought them into the courtroom. I did my research on lawyers, but I did not do my research on courthouses. Knowing what I know now, I would have filed at a different courthouse. The system let me down.

Forgiving the system was not easy because the system is so huge.

> "The weak can never forgive. Forgiveness is
> the attribute of the strong."—Gandhi

> "Forgiveness is not always easy. At times, it feels
> more painful than the wound we suffered, to forgive
> the one that inflicted it. And yet, there is no peace
> without forgiveness."—Marianne Williamson

77

Mission Statement—Oprah says she believes everyone needs a mission statement. It seems to have worked for her, so I wrote one. I believe it can help you stay on track in your truth. Start with something, and you can always add and change it until you get clear on who you are and what you want. This is mine:

I am in charge of my life. I take charge now. I keep my life organized and clear of litter. I move through life's changes and challenges with ease, peace, and calm, knowing that spirit guides me. I am secure enough to enjoy success. I am secure enough to learn from and accept my mistakes and failures. I am a compassionate woman in touch with my passion. I laugh and enjoy life. I am a woman of strength, physically, emotionally, spiritually, and mentally. I take care of myself. I honor my mind, body, and spirit. I seek to do what is best for me. I follow my passion and honor who I am. I am open to gratefully and graciously receiving my bounty. I am a good friend and sensitive companion. I am a woman who is not afraid to stand up for what

I know to be true. I am a woman who gives back and is not afraid to ask for help. I am a complete person whose spirit is whole and beautiful. I live in a feeling of oneness with all of creation.

78

Women Supporting Women—I grew up thinking men had the real jobs. I did not think women had a very palpable role in life; frankly, I do not believe I had any respect for women. With no respect for women, how could I respect myself? I began to look for the heroine in women and now see us as the truly strong and beautiful beings we are. Women create and sustain life. You cannot get more powerful than that. I now believe that women do not have "penis envy," as Sigmund Freud would have had us believe, but rather that men have "uterus envy." They cannot grow a whole human being who can be born, grow up, talk, walk, go to school, and drive a car. Wow!

If you are a man reading this I assure you there are men who need to get together and feel supported. Feeling unsupported and alone does not know gender.

79

Listen to Other Women Tell their Stories—During my divorce, I received many e-mails from women who were having some of the same struggles as I was with divorce. I shared the information I had obtained from my research and experience. All women have a story to tell. Let us listen to and honor each others' stories. We must stand together strong and support each other if we are to get anywhere near equality. Many people say the right words, but we do not have many right actions. The good, strong, secure, and loving men will support us. Together we can build a world of peace and beauty where all life is honored. All life seeks homeostasis or balance. Let us work together to that end.

80

Heroes—Heroes and positive role models are important at all ages. I have always had heroes, but as I grow, they change. I can remember when Leo Tolstoy and Ben Franklin were my heroes. Fortunately, I have grown, and my new heroes are mostly women. I need women role models because I want to be the best woman I can be. Here are just a few of my women heroes: Joan Kroc, Louise L. Hay, Oprah, Maya Anjelou, Beth Henley, Alanis Morissette, Shirley MacLaine, Sheryl Crow, Cathy Rigby, Elizabeth Smart, Goldie Hawn, Bette Midler, Bonnie Raitt, Barbara Walters, Nora Jones, Dolly Parton, Linda Evans, Jane Curtin, Betty White, Mary Chapin Carpenter, Rita Coolidge, Cyndi Lauper, Katie Couric, Elaine Pagels, Candace Pert, Reba McEntire, Penny Marshall, Madeleine Albright, Barbra Streisand, Maria Shriver, Rev. Lauren Artress, Angela Lansbury, J. K. Rowling, Jean Shinoda Bolen, Marianne Williamson, Nora Ephron, Indra Devi, Janet L. Robinson, Arianna Huffington, Margaret Starbird, Kim Campbell, Whoopi Goldberg, Eve Ensler, Julia Cameron, Sherry Lansing, Heidi Klum, Judy Collins, Diane Sawyer, Ellen DeGeneres, Toni Morrison, Gayle King, Meredith Vieira, Helen Mirren, Dawn French, and my mom. There are thousands of wonderful, beautiful, talented women who deserve to be everyone's heroine. Since I look for the specialness in people, I like almost everyone. I admire most writers, directors, instructors, mothers, and anyone who takes pride in what they do. Those who take pride in what they do shine, and I feel their light. I'm not mentioning friends and family members who are my heroes in case I omit someone very deserving. My aunts, cousins, sister, sister-in-law, nieces, and what I call "shirttail relations" are all so awesome and inspiring. Every woman has her story. I truly salute women everywhere. I honor their stories. I do not know everything about the women I have mentioned. However, I know certain things about them that appeal to me. Every day I hear of, read about, or just remember someone I would like to add to my list.

Men, I also salute you and honor your stories. There are many men who inspire me, but for this exercise I wanted to get in touch with the feminine. Men, make your list of men who inspire you to be the best man you can be.

I have to laugh at myself when I look at my list of men because near the top of the list is Willie Nelson. I love him and his musical talent. I have had the good fortune of seeing many talented performers. Here are a few of my men whom I have found interesting and talented: Michael Jackson, Deepak Chopra, John Denver, Gandhi, Nat King Cole, Sidney Poitier, Marvin Gaye, George Lucas, Joseph Campbell, Richard Branson, Stephen King, Tom Hanks, Dr. Oz, Leo Tolstoy, Ben Franklin, John Adams, Tyler Perry, Dr. Chopra, Dr. Weil, and Jimmy Fallon. Make your list, think about the talents your heroes have and how this relates to you. You may begin to realize that you have more talent than you are using. Looking for the hero in others enhances my work and my life. I hope you find the hero in yourself. I find it fun to find the talent and uniqueness in everyone.

81

Being Perfect—You are perfect! You are the perfect person for your life's lessons and what you are to give to the world. I have mentioned heroes and role models not because you should strive to be exactly like them, but because I want you to recognize your own gifts. It is amazing but true that what you admire in others, you have in yourself, but maybe you haven't realized it yet or haven't begun to fine tune or embrace that gift.

As I mentioned before, Leo Tolstoy and Benjamin Franklin were my heroes. The sad part is the reason that they were important to me. They strived for perfection as human beings. They would make lists of what was necessary for a perfect person, but after a week or two when it became obvious they could not achieve that perfection, they would drink and get wild. Later they would try again.

I have learned that being a good person with good intentions and forgiving myself when I am not "perfect" is a healthier way to live. I love that I now see perfection and growth in my missteps and mistakes. My mother used to say that the only person who makes no mistakes is a dead person.

"When you realize how perfect everything is you will tilt your head back and laugh at the sky."—Buddha

82

Take risks—Taking risks means you are okay with falling down or failing. You are strong, can get up, dust yourself off, and start all over again. I am a risk taker. As I get older, my risk taking is a little calmer because as an older person I want to protect myself from physical pain. However, I am so proud of myself that I was not afraid of pain or making mistakes when I was younger. I still am not afraid of failure. I have found most of my failures amusing. I think I am so very funny. I laugh at myself often. My failures, my decorating style, and things I do are hilarious. I do not take myself seriously, and I believe life is meant to be lived fully. I intend to live it to the fullest, and I cannot do that without making mistakes. This makes me limitless.

One of my favorite stories is when I wrote a song for the first dance at my wedding. I decided I could write lyrics and found a collaborator who put my lyrics to music. I heard my words to music and thought I was awesome. I found a bandleader who wrote the music and did a demo of this song for my wedding. Someone asked me what made me think I could write a song, and a friend replied, "She does not know she can't." I believe I can do whatever I want, and I will try almost anything. I am not afraid to look silly because I like myself when I am silly. When my life is ending and I can no longer do much, I want to sit in my chair, feeling pleased and full of myself with all of my experiences. My experiences and stories about risk taking and letting go of fears all fill my spirit to the brim. Oh, do I have stories!

"For me, the safest place is out on a limb."—Shirley MacLaine

"Only those who dare to fail greatly can ever achieve greatly."—Robert F. Kennedy

83

Gratitude—I currently live in gratitude in a house I love in my hometown of Alpena, Michigan. I work out of my home doing massage for people and horses. I also have clients who come to me for birthing classes and others I attend to at their deliveries as a labor doula. Now and then I officiate at a wedding. I have a cute, little black puppy named Tara. My precious Julie dog passed away just before I left San Diego. I am grateful for the sixteen and a half years she shared with me. I have a kayak and sit on the river enjoying the beauty around me. I have relatives up and down the river whom I often visit from my kayak. The local college has great instructors and interesting classes, which I usually take at least one of each semester. I have started a novel and to say I am happy is putting it mildly. I have enjoyed quality time with my mother and learned so much about myself and life.

I highly recommend the tools I used because I am happy. I feel so blessed and continue to see all that happens in my life as a gift. I say a gratitude list every morning and any other time I have a special moment.

If you need some help with this part of your journey

Simple Abundance Journal of Gratitude by Sarah Ban Breathnach is a favorite.

> "When you are grateful fear disappears and abundance appears."—Anthony Robbins

84

Passion—In life it is important to find what sets you on fire. I have known many women who are only looking for a man to set them on fire. They become lost and depressed when the fire goes out and the man departs. They have created nothing else in their lives to fulfill their spirits. Some also put all their fire in their jobs and, again, if it goes wrong they are devastated. Life requires balance. We must have many kinds of interests that we can put our passion into. When we think of these things, we smile and our eyes light up. I worked for one company for over fourteen years and had planned to be there until I was too old to get to work. I put my heart and soul into my work and gave 100 percent every day. One day I received a telegram saying my job had been eliminated. I turned on the television to find out the company had filed for bankruptcy and the doors were closed. It took me awhile to figure out who I was as a person because I had totally identified with my job. I had no clue what to do next.

The only thing I had going for me was my total faith that the situation was a gift to put me in a better place. I have always felt guided. My task now was to keep knocking on doors until I found the one that opened, the door I was supposed to enter next in my life's quest. I continue to put passion in all I do. Neither my job ending nor my marriage failing was a sign for me to close down my passion for anything in life. Experiences are lessons to teach us how to open up in a healthy way to healthy events and people.

After writing this, I had the pleasure of discovering a group called "Women on Fire." I attended one of their conferences in my hometown. A group of women with a dream put this together, and it surpassed their wildest dreams; women came from miles away to join together and spark each other. The age range was twelve to eighty-nine. I was introduced to the conference by amazing women who asked me to join them. When I got home I felt so light, I was filled with peace, and I had energy to write. I wondered why I felt so light, and then I realized that the women I was with were so strong that I was able to just enjoy and did not need to attend to anyone else's needs. As a lifetime server (who was an excellent flight attendant), I tend to serve people in some fashion wherever I go. That day I was free. Thank you, ladies!

"Passion is energy. Feel the power that comes from focusing on what excites you."—Oprah Winfrey

85

Pride—Many women are afraid to be full of themselves. When I was young, parents used to spank children for being full of themselves. I hope times are changing and we are realizing that a generation of people with no self-esteem did not serve anyone well.

One day, while watching a dog show on television, I happened to catch the interview with the winning dog's owner. They asked her the secret to raising a winner, and she replied, "I never say no. I believe to raise a champion they must never hear the word *no*." This stunned me because when you see a child in the store or at someone's home, one of the first words they say is *no* along with a vigorous head shake.

Why do we not raise our children to be champions? A child's attention span is so short that, instead of being dramatic with the word *no*, we could take a moment and direct the child's interest to something positive. We can teach them that *yes, they can.* Our children will grow up to be champions. This also means that if we direct ourselves to things we can do, we too can become champions.

85

The Internal Critic—The critical voice we heard as a child can often still be heard like a recording in our heads. We think it is our own inner voice and that it makes sense. We listen and let it lead us because it is so familiar.

Just the other day I observed a young lady muttering negative statements to herself. I said excuse me but you are bulling yourself. You are being cruel to your own little self. I made her step into my bathroom and stand in front of the mirror where I coached her to say some kind statements and promise to support herself kindly.

It is time to start a life of kindness to yourself. If the voice you hear is not kind and positive, you must tell it to step back. That goes for the inner critic and any outer critics. We usually attract others who treat us like we treat ourselves. Speak kindly to yourself and attract others who do the same.

It is also important to note that the internal critic is great at shutting you down and sabotaging you. Therefore it is important to catch the inner critic's voice, and then you can learn to shut it down before it shuts you down. Many people are so use to beating themselves up that they do not recognize the negative voice.

86

Anger—Anger is the main reason I wrote this book. I read in the news about people who shot their spouses, ran them over with a car, and took other drastic measures that put them in jail and destroyed many lives. Anger is an emotion that we can learn to express in constructive ways. With self-awareness we can get to the deep source of the power behind the anger. Since our anger is a part of us, it cannot be ignored or denied. Pretending it does not exist or trying to shove it down with food, alcohol, shopping, or any other method, will only magnify the issue. Seek help. Find someone who understands the importance of rescuing the part of yourself that is so angry. You do not want to deny any part of yourself even if it is socially unacceptable. Love, accept, and heal all parts of yourself.

I remember seeing my ex-husband when I was driving through a strip mall and the thought of stepping on the gas crossed my mind. I did not want my precious self to be punished for a moment of unconscious behavior, however. I want to live consciously, in peace. I also knew my anger was really not at him but at myself for falling prey to him. I had to heal myself so as not to fall prey to anyone or anything, including my own ignorance. I educated myself about me and my behavior.

I truly believe in the 111 steps in this book. Anger is like steam in a pressure cooker. Screaming in your car as you drive down the freeway is perfect. Building something with a hammer and nails or just pounding nails into a board will work. It is important to understand that anger is like built-up pressure that needs to be released. Journaling about this pressure can help you understand its source. Anger usually comes from past experiences; the current issue is just the straw that breaks the camel's back.

"Anger is an acid that can do more harm to
the vessel in which it is stored than to anything
on which it is poured."—Mark Twain

87

The Sympathetic Nervous System—When I write about the wonderful things you can do for yourself, such as massage, breathing, visualizing, petting your dog or cat, walking in nature, or doing yoga, I'm referring to the parasympathetic nervous system. The parasympathetic nervous system is in the right side of the brain and is best known for controlling rest and digestion. The opposite is the sympathetic nervous system, which the left side of the brain controls; this is better known as the fight or flight response. The body prepares for fight or flight by halting digestion, elevating blood pressure, and dilating the eyes.

Unfortunately, it seems to me that most people are in fight or flight all day, every day. Their bodies are on alert twenty-four hours a day. As you can imagine, that is stressful for the body. When the body is stressed, the adrenal glands release cortisol, which suppresses the immune system. Add eating lots of meat, which stimulates acid in the body, and you end up with a body that is distressed and ripe for "dis-ease."

Logic would suggest that by eating lots of fruits and vegetables, limiting red meat, learning to breathe, and having a balance of exercise and relaxation, we can prepare our bodies for a long and healthy life.

Relationships— Life is about relationships. We must be able to establish a healthy relationship with nature, the earth, God, animals, community, family, self, and all of life. I have met so many women who feel they cannot live without a man, and they go from relationship to relationship. Some women will stay in abusive relationships because they do not want to change their lifestyles; they feel they cannot make it on their own, or they feel they deserve abuse.

I am confused by the woman who is only charming and witty when a man is around. With women she is blah and snarly. She is only comfortable with male relationships. Some women want to be comfortable with male relationships and spend their time waiting for Mr. Right; they may miss out on life.

Some men are totally preoccupied with women. They only know how to have a relationship with women while pursuing them.

Many people feel empty and lonely when they are not in lover relationships. They are always looking for someone to fill their lives with purpose, entertainment and a myriad of other gifts that can only be found within oneself. Therefore, they are always left wanting.

It is impossible to have a healthy relationship with someone else if you cannot have a healthy relationship with yourself.

89

Congruency—Most people are fractured. That is why we need to pull ourselves together to create wholeness. One must accept all of one's fractured parts. If you have a love-hate relationship with yourself, you will most likely attract a partner with whom you also end up having a love-hate relationship.

I have also found that the love-hate feeling and incongruence within oneself can lead to illness. The inner struggle or battle can cause illness. This is most likely a love-hate feeling for oneself which carries over to others. It is important to identify your inner battles and make peace. These incongruence's can manifest themselves in many ways.

The incongruence can be something like saying, "I hate people who lie," but then telling a lie. It could also be saying, "I cannot abide stealing," but then taking home pencils or office items from work.

> "The life of inner peace, being harmonious and without stress is the easiest type of existence."—Norman Vincent Peale

90

Control—Sometimes when we feel we are losing control of a situation, we react. It is important to act with consciousness instead of to react. Emotions can cause us to react crazily. That is another reason why the 111 steps in this book are so important. Whenever I felt myself wanting to react, I immediately used the steps that kept me calm and sane. I would immediately go for a walk, sit in the hot tub, go to a bookstore, or meditate on a beach or mountain. I believe in the process of this book. I am proud of myself for using these steps; I am creating a better life for myself rather than getting stuck in a deep, dark abyss of anger, regret, and revenge.

Some of the hardest people to watch out for are controllers. They usually start out gradually and build. Their techniques vary only slightly. They make awesome actors as they use pity and anger to get their way. They find fault with your friends and family. They work to make you feel you are nothing without them. Beware of anyone who belittles you or makes you feel small. Beware of anyone who does not support your goals and independence. Run; do not walk.

I was very surprised to hear from numerous other

women and men that before a breakup or when the cheating began, their spouses or significant others were finding fault with them.

> "We're so engaged in doing things to achieve purpose of outer value that we forget the inner value, the rapture that is associated with being alive is what it is all about."—Joseph Campbell

91

Boundaries—It is intriguing how many people do not have boundaries or truly understand what they are. Boundaries are your safe space. Establish what your safe space is and just say "no." Touching anything on my desk, expecting me to not put my mother and dog first, expecting to move in with me, expecting me to quit my work, expecting me not to travel, having expectations of me without asking me first...these break my boundaries and will not be tolerated. Boundaries will help your soul, spirit, heart, and body feel safe. Before you date again, it is important to know your boundaries. Anyone who does not respect your boundaries probably has none of his or her own and is trouble. I will not be intimidated into doing anything or going anywhere that does not fit my belief system. My belief system keeps me feeling safe, happy, and healthy.

92

Compassion—Since I worked through the steps in this book, I found a gentle, loving side of myself that is very compassionate. I looked at the underlying reasons I got where I was, and I had enormous compassion for myself. I do not believe you can have compassion for others until you have compassion for yourself. You have heard "do unto others as you would have them do unto you." I believe most people do just that. They are critical and judgmental of themselves, and critical and judgmental of others.

I have worked with people who had a huge weight loss and are judgmental of those who are struggling with their weight. I then know they are not finished with the gift of their weight. They have no compassion for the part of themselves that gained the weight. It is important to love all parts of yourself and have compassion for yourself. When you do, you will be ready to have a healthy relationship with yourself and others.

> "If you want others to be happy, practice
> compassion. If you want to be happy,
> practice compassion."—Dalai Lama

93

Comfort in Your Skin—There is nothing more beautiful than watching someone move who is comfortable in his or her skin. It doesn't matter whether they are male or female, large or small. I have had the pleasure of watching people of all sizes and heights move with grace and inner power that is captivating. When I had a good figure, I felt it was not good enough, and now I would give anything for that figure. My measurements used to be 24-36-24 and I weighed 110 pounds, yet I was criticized if I gained a pound or two. I remember having lunch and some people saying, "You could stand to lose a few pounds." In other words, "Don't go feeling good about yourself—you could be better."

Now past sixty years of age, I will weigh whatever I want. As a flight attendant I was weighed in like cattle for slaughter. It was very demeaning to get on the scale and be judged for thirty years. I had a roommate who was fired for being one-fourth of a pound overweight. Since weight was always such a serious issue during those years, I refuse to let it be one now. I am very comfortable with my size and very happy in my skin.

It is important to be okay with yourself and with what you see in the mirror. Those who would criticize you are most likely not happy with themselves.

94

Focus and Mindfulness—I find life amusing. I amuse myself every day. My feet have no arch, so if I get carried away when walking downstairs, I will fall. I can fall just from walking down the street; sprained ankles have been with me since I was a child. I now know that if I walk consciously and mindfully in life, I will not fall or damage my ankles. Being emotionally to high or too low can cause me to fall or have an incident in my life.

Also, if I lose focus and do not move through life mindfully I miss hearing the inner voice and then make huge mistakes that cost me. How many times have you not listened to the inner voice and wished you had? Instead, we sit in a mess and say, "I knew it." We did but it is too late.

One day I was going down the street and a car ran into me. She was clearly at fault. My inner voice said, "Do not move the car." A fire truck came and was directing traffic and I asked the fireman if I should move my car. I was totally ignoring the inner voice. The fireman told me to go ahead. Now my car was in a bicycle lane and I got the ticket from the policewoman. Fortunately for me my insurance company understood and saw that no matter how you looked at it, it was not my fault. However, I did pay for not listening to my inner voice. I had to pay the ticket.

95

Sex and Money—I address sex and money together because they usually go together; these two make prostitutes of almost everyone in the world. I am amazed at how much power they have. Sex and money make the world go round. My goal is that they do not make *my* world go round. I want my world to be guided by my heart and soul. Sex and money as currency can be soul depleting.

Some people feel that all they have to offer is their bodies, while others feel all they have to offer is money. If that is what you are offering and seeking approval for, I guarantee you will have trouble in life and feel worthless.

We are all like multi-faceted diamonds. When you begin to value all of your facets you will also appreciate the value of the facets in other diamonds.

96

Your Identity—Take time to think about how you want to be identified. Defining who you are is important before you go back to dating because you will attract what you are putting out into the world. If you are a phony you will attract the same. Knowing your identity and standing steadfast in that identity will help keep the undesirables away.

Do not let others define you. When you spend time with yourself and know who you are, no one can tell you otherwise. My ex-husband used to tell me what I was thinking. He was so far off that I knew he had no clue who I was. I refused to be who he was trying to make me be. I would not react because I knew this would lead to more control and abuse.

I would walk away and go find a way to make myself feel strong inside. I think that is how I stayed sane. I did the techniques in this book. I knew I could not change anyone else, but I could work on myself and see where that took me. I wanted to survive.

97

Believe in Yourself—Confidence and a belief in yourself are crucial to success in your life. Who do you know who has the confidence you wish you had? Think of them and practice the feeling they give off. Fake it until you make it.

Dr. Chopra says, "Success is the expansion of happiness."

98

Mirrors—I love working with mirrors. While working with a group of cancer patients, I passed out hand mirrors and asked everyone to look into their mirror and say, "I love you." It was amazing how many people cannot do this. Mirrors are multi-dimensional and powerful for self-healing work. Remember that life is multi-dimensional. Use the mirrors for positive statements to keep on track. Identify some of your dimensions and learn to love and accept them. You will then begin to love the whole you.

99

Depression—I am not a doctor, so I am not telling anyone with major depression what to do. I am simply saying that in my experience depression can be very creative. I like to delve into depression and use it to elicit creativity. Creativity is often buried beneath pain. When we open up and allow ourselves to feel, we can unearth talent and possibilities.

Sometimes I use it for a day off. Taking a day to stay in your PJ's, eat popcorn, and watch movies can be therapeutic and the best time to journal, work through pains and create.

100

Expectations—Expectations can be a setup for failure. What you expect of yourself, your spouse, your friends, your boss, or your life will very likely set you up for disappointment. Be open, free, accepting, and allowing of everyone and your life. J. K. Rowling said she never in her wildest dreams thought her book would become the success it did. She just created, wrote, and let it go. Freedom allowed her writing to grow beyond what she could imagine. The same is true of relationships; if you allow them to be, they can grow and flourish. Control and fear will smother and kill most relationships and creativity.

101

Surrender—Surrender to life and love. If you surrender to relationships, the possibilities are endless. Webster's dictionary definition of surrender is *to give up possession of or power over.* Surrendering can be difficult for many people. You will need to practice. When you find yourself hanging onto an idea or opinion, just stop a moment and surrender. Take time to notice how you feel. Ideally, you will feel lighter. If you do not feel lighter, you will need to look at some of your fears. What is the worst that can happen?

I realized that my biggest fear was to get divorced. After I had been granted a divorce I was still alive and the only change was that a person who did not enhance my life was gone. I was free to create a new life. I realized that if I let fear take over I would seek comfort in the known. I would end up in a similar situation. I had been there and it was horrible; I was not about to go back. I would go into the unknown. I was ready for the next adventure, the next stage of my life.

I have also noticed that surrender works on little things. If I decide I want something I can look, hope and wait but as soon as I let it go...it comes to me.

102

Change—Many people do not like change. Without change, you have no growth. You may notice that everywhere you go you like to sit in the same seat or at the same table. I notice in my yoga class that everyone likes to put his or her mat in the place at each class they attend. We like our routines and thrive on them. I am not saying you have to get rid of all your routines, but try to experiment with taking a different seat or table, or putting your mat in a different spot. When life hits you with change, instead of panicking, realize it is an opportunity for growth. Those who take this attitude will tell you unbelievable stories of awesome gain from unexpected change. Change is your friend.

"If you change the way you look at things, the things you look at change."—Wayne Dyer

103

Trust—Trust becomes a big issue if we feel betrayed when a relationship does not turn out as we dreamed. Usually we say this mistrust is with the opposite sex, but internally the mistrust is with ourselves. We feel we made a mistake last time with our choices and might do it again. The thought of going through the pain again causes us to put up walls. If we go into a new relationship, we go in with walls and of course attract someone else with walls. We will keep making the same mistakes until we take time to examine what happened, learn new lessons, and make changes. In the end, you will have to trust yourself and take a risk. The good news is you just keep getting better.

I find that I can trust myself if I take time to sit with myself in silence. Then I act rather than react. This makes me feel confident as I move forward.

104

Date Again—If you have done the other 103 steps you are now almost ready to date again. I took one and a half years of working on all the steps before I was ready to consider dating. It is important to let go of the old. Sometimes we become addicted to the pain because it is familiar. It is time to get addicted to happiness and make it your norm. Start small with coffee dates and lunch. Take your time and work up to evening dates. If you are like me, dating again can feel very scary in the beginning. Listen to your senses. My stomach told me whenever I was near anyone like my ex.

I met a very handsome and sexy man with whom I had a great relationship for ten years. When our relationship ended, I moved from San Diego to my hometown in Michigan to care for my aging mother, to write, and to begin the next chapter of my life. I have no fear of making changes in my life now. I trust that life will take me where I need to be.

I feel I have lots of love to give and my heart is open to receive. Dating, friendships, and love will continue to be in my life.

105

Compliments—Now that you know the awesome you, be prepared to accept compliments. Just say "thank you," smile, and allow yourself to marinate in the compliment.

106

Definition of Love—Love means something different to everyone. Take time to sit with yourself and write down your definition of love. Be prepared to discuss what you think love is and what you want it to be in your life. Know what you are willing to give. It is important to be honest in a relationship about what you need and what the deal breakers are. Notice how a person treats you because that is usually their definition of love.

As with compassion, if you cannot love yourself, you cannot love someone else. You have probably heard that before, but now you need to get this information from your head to your heart. Make a list of all your good points. Write down everything about yourself that you like. Look at yourself as you would a stranger. I have seen people who were very loved by family and friends, yet they felt lonely and unloved. This always puzzles me. People cut themselves off from feeling love. Let your love shine and feel the love of others.

107

Open Your Heart—Many times when love dies or we feel betrayed, we want to shut down. We think that if we don't open our hearts, then we can't be hurt. We cheat ourselves out of growth and the opportunity to find new love. Physically, my heart is an organ that pumps blood through my body. Emotionally, my heart represents my expression of feelings. I want to take care of it physically and emotionally. Shutting it down or ignoring its pain will not keep it healthy or help with healthy relationships. Awareness is a major key to health in all aspects of our lives. I put my hands on my heart, and I ask "Are you ready for a new relationship?" I then relax and feel my body's response. Does my body cringe? Or does it sigh and breathe? It sounds silly, but communicating with yourself and with all of life will open your heart and spirit to what is good and true for you.

108

Maintain Independence—You can allow love in your life and still be independent. If you have done the other 107 steps, you have enough self-realization to have a healthy relationship with a partner, family, community, and yourself. Never forget who you are or your value as an individual.

If you put yourself and your God first, your partner second, children third, family fourth, and community fifth, your life will have the proper balance to be whole. Each in the sequence will then support the other and create a stable foundation. If you have a good relationship with your God and yourself, that relationship will support your partnership. If you have a good relationship with your God, yourself, and your partner, you will have a strong foundation for your children. If you have a good relationship with yourself, God, partner, and children, you will have a good foundation for your family and other relatives. If you have a good relationship with yourself, God, partner, children, and family, you will have a good foundation for a strong community. The love and care will trickle down.

109

Allow—My favorite word in the world is *allow*. I allowed myself to turn the pain of broken dreams and promises into a gift of growth and new beginnings. I allowed myself the luxury of surrendering to life. I allowed myself to be okay with not being perfect.

I continue to allow life to change and happen. If I maintained an attachment to my ex, dreams of who he was, or dreams of what our life could have been, I would be trapped in misery. I could not let fear of the unknown keep me trapped and attached to this man. I must set myself free and allow the universe to bring me a new life.

I now endeavor to always be free. I look out at the world and allow it to bring me new joy every day. I allow the old to fall away and the new to be explored. I am okay with change.

110

Should— *Should* is one of the nastiest words in the English language. It causes people to put pressure on themselves that can be unrealistic. *Should* can sink or kill your spirit faster than a speeding bullet. When people come to me for a massage, I feel *should* on their shoulders; sometimes it feels so heavy it weakens their backs.

Avoid it at all costs. Do not *should* on yourself. Catch it and rephrase it. Use gentle words that allow you to have peace and a "can do" attitude. You cannot change the past, but you have full control of your life now. Be kind to yourself with your language. Notice how your body feels when you rephrase a *should* statement. You will love the feeling and learn what loving yourself feels like.

111

My Shining Light—I took a class in astronomy and learned that stars shine because they reflect light from the sun. My goal is to reflect light from God. My prayer is always "Thank you, God, for allowing me to be a vessel of your love, light, and healing." Let your light shine. Together we will light up the world.

I wish you all a wealth of love, light, health, and happiness.

"We don't receive wisdom; we must discover it for ourselves after a journey that no one can take for us or spare us." —Marcel Proust

This is a copy of the labyrinth at Chartres. Get quiet, and using a finger from your dominant and/ or non-dominant hand, follow the path from outside to the center, then back out again.

The labyrinth calms the mind and helps you find answers. You will probably find that there is a labyrinth you can walk in your town. The Grace Cathedral website (gracecathedral. org) has a list of most labyrinths in the United States.

Enjoy!

GayFry@aol.com
www.gayfry.com

Gay Lyn Fry, H.H.P., C.H.T., CD (Doula, nurturing women during labor and childbirth), hypnotherapist and hypnosis instructor, hypnosis For birthing and CAPPA childbirth educator, RYT (registered yoga instructor), naturopathic doctor, California state certified instructor and holistic health practitioner, Reiki master, and certified labyrinth facilitator (Grace Cathedral trained).

Gay Lyn began her studies in the healthcare field while finishing up a thirty-year career as an international flight attendant. Her pursuit of therapies to assist her clients led her to study many modalities with many well-known doctors, teachers, and healers. She has taught Reiki, massage, couples massage, mind-body healing, pregnancy massage, yoga teacher certification, soul retrieval, shamanic journeying, hypnosis and dog massage. She has also served as a volunteer Doula at a major medical facility as well as a doula and Hypnobirthing childbirth educator. She taught yoga at the gym in her neighborhood in San Diego where she had a loyal following for many years. As a naturopathic doctor, she enjoyed the study of yoga as medicine at the Naturopathic and Yogic Science Institute in Bangalore, India. As a labyrinth facilitator, she has facilitated labyrinth walks for The Learning Annex and First United Methodist Church, among others. A week-long stay in Chartres, France where she walked the labyrinth revealed to her the ongoing power of labyrinths. Bookstores and other venues have enjoyed Gay Lyn's various workshops. Currently, she is working on her writing projects and doing massage on humans and horses. She also continues to help women to have peaceful, powerful birth experiences. A passionate person, she believes very much in yoga, massage, hypnosis, the mind-body connection, and working with mothers, fathers, newborns, and labyrinths. She feels empowered by her work and seeks to empower others.

Drawing Exercises

Draw yourself doing what you love.

Draw yourself now, then draw yourself as
the person you want to be.

Draw a picture of yourself happy.

After you have drawn your pictures, notice the colors you
have chosen. Notice any and all details you have put in
your pictures. Sit with your pictures and let them talk
to you. Keep the pictures in your mind and get in the
positive feelings. Remember, where the mind goes, the
energy flows.

Notes

Notes

Notes

Notes